EVERY HYMN HAS A S

Volume 4

John Large

Published by

John Large, 6 Church Lane, Hundleby, Spilsby, Lincs. PE23 5NA

CONTENTS

3

For the healing of the nations
GRAHAM KENDRICK   1950-   158
Beauty for brokenness

EDMUND SPENSER
"Most glorious Lord of life, that on this day"

Edmund Spenser was the greatest of those poets whose genius dazzled the final generation of the reign of Elizabeth I – with one massive exception. William Shakespeare was in his prime when Spenser was living out his final years in poverty. Spenser has one hymn that is still to be found in many of the modern hymnals, but his lasting memorial to the end of time is his magnificent work 'The Faerie Queene'.

The events of his life are somewhat obscure, as indeed is the case with Shakespeare. But we do know that he was born probably in 1552 in the Smithfield area of London. He was descended from a good family, an offshoot of the Allthorpes. John, his father, was probably one of the Spensers of Hurstwood, near Burnley, but at the time of Edmund's birth he had fallen on hard times and was working as a journeyman cloth-maker.

Edmund was clearly an unusually clever boy, so was able to gain a place at Merchant Taylors' School. From there he went up to Pembroke Hall, Cambridge, as a sizar scholar, receiving tuition in return for certain menial duties. While at college he started contributing sonnets to the London periodicals.

After taking his BA and MA degrees he spent some time in the north where he wrote his first work of note, 'The Shepherd's Calendar', a series of twelve pastorals. It is a difficult work to read because of his fondness for medieval words and phrases, and a rustic familiarity of expression that in places is virtually dialect. But the work did gain for him immediate attention from the literary world. Even at this early stage of his career he had started work on his great epic, 'The Faerie Queene'.

In 1578, when he was 26, he became secretary to John Young, Bishop of Rochester. The following year Gabriel Harvey, a literary friend from his Cambridge days, introduced him to the all-powerful Earl of Leicester, and he took up a position in the Earl's household.

There he met Leicester's nephew, Sir Philip Sidney, which was the start close friendship. Sidney was no mean poet himself, but the friendship cut tragically short in 1586. Queen Elizabeth had previously refused t him leave her Court, where he was a charmer both to Her Majesty and m others, but when Leicester led an army to the Netherlands against Spanish, Raleigh was given command of the cavalry.

He led three successful charges but was finally felled by a musket embedding itself in his thigh. He was led from the field in great agony, was about to drink a draught of water when he saw a soldier lying man on the ground, longingly gazing at the bottle. Sir Philip passed it untasted, exclaiming "Thy need is greater than mine!" Spenser wro memorable elegy on his friend, which he called 'Astrophel'. Sidney only 32 at the time of his death, two years younger than Spenser.

In 1580 Spenser went to Ireland as secretary to Lord Grey of Wilton, had just taken up the position of Lord Deputy of Ireland. He immortal his employer by characterising him as Artegal, the personification of justi

Lord Grey's stay in Ireland was very short, but he made his secretary C of the Irish Court of Chancery, for which he received the lucrative lease abbey lands in County Wexford. These he sold for a tidy sum.

In 1586 he was awarded another mammoth piece of bounty, 3,000 acre County Cork, on which stood Kilcolman Castle. There, beside his belo river, the Mulla, he wrote most of his great work, 'The Faerie Queene'.

By 1589 the first three books were completed. Spenser's plan was for work to consist of twelve books in all, epitomising the twelve moral virt but it is unlikely that he completed more than six. The first three, which v considered the finest, were on Holiness, Temperance and Chastity.

Spenser invited his good friend Sir Walter Raleigh over to Kilcolman in 1 and showed him the three completed books. Raleigh, who was a fine po his own right, persuaded his friend to return to England with him and s the work to the Queen. She was flattered by the effusive references to he and granted Spenser an annual pension of £150 from the public purse. following year the books were published in London.

In 1591, when Spenser was still only 39, he published a volume of shorter poems, quaintly entitled 'Complaints'. He was in fact rather fond of complaining, which seems rather unreasonable of him considering how generously he was treated by his patrons.

Four years later, Spenser published 'Colin Clout's Come Home Again' which contains some very beautiful verse. It has many allusions to his own personal life, including the story of his visit to London with Raleigh. In the same year, 1595, he also published 'Epithalamion', a fine work showing great mastery of composition. He wrote it at the residence of the Earl of Essex, and it was a celebration in verse of his recent marriage to Elizabeth Boyle.

A year later, working at his Kilcolman estate, he completed books four, five and six of 'The Faerie Queene', the legends of Friendship, Justice and Courtesy. The final six books required for completing his grand design are traditionally supposed to have been lost overboard on a voyage to England, but it is unlikely that they were ever written.

He also wrote a prose work, 'A View of the Present State of Ireland', a book of some wisdom if his views were somewhat preconceived. It is at any rate a fine example of old English prose.

In 1598 Spenser was appointed Sheriff of Cork, a position that caused him to be a political target and led to tragedy. Almost at once Tyrone's rebellion broke out, and Kilcolman Castle was burnt to the ground, probably by the O'Neills. Their new-born child died in the pandemonium, but Spenser and his wife managed to escape to London with their other two children. They took lodgings in King Street, Westminster, which was then a poor area of the city.

Edmund Spenser never recovered from the trauma of the attack on his Irish home, and he died at his London lodgings in January of the following year. According to Ben Jonson the main cause of his death was poverty. In view of their affluent lifestyle in Ireland, the amount of work he published towards the end of his life, the esteem in which poets were held in the time of Elizabeth I and his wealthy friends and patrons, this seems incredible.

The Earl of Essex paid for a lavish funeral, and he was buried with s style in Westminster Abbey. His tomb lies next to his hero and inspira Geoffrey Chaucer. Twenty years later a monument to him was erecte Lady Anne Clifford, whose inscription read: "The Prince of Poets o time." He can justly claim to have inspired the poetry of Milton and Kea later years.

The spirit of Edmund Spenser's poetry came from the older poetr England, the chivalrous ideas of the Middle Ages with its fantastic im and its constant use of allegory. His poetical form was influenced by Italian studies, and resulted in a polished and elaborate style w resurrected once again the world of chivalry.

He makes constant use of imagery in a manner so beautiful that an age fu poets looked up to him as master of the noble art. His scenes and fig entrance the reader by a spell every bit as powerful as those of the encha and elves amidst whom we are surrounded when we read his poetry.

Three years before his death he wrote 'Fowre Hymns', of which designed for Sundays, is still to be found in many hymnals. The first v reads:

> "Most glorious Lord of life, that on this day
> Didst make thy triumph over death and sin,
> And having harrowed hell, didst bring away
> Captivity thence captive, us to win."

It is normally sung to the tune 'Farley Castle', which is also sometimes for Thomas Ken's hymn "Her Virgin eyes saw God incarnate born." tune was composed by Henry Lawes, born in 1596, three years be Spenser's death. He was the official composer at Court and wrote Coronation anthem for Charles II, as well as composing tunes for a number of hymns, some still to be found in more traditional hymnals.

Like John Darwall, Lawes composed tunes for the psalms, some of w have been transposed into hymn tunes. His melody for Psalm 32 is sometimes used for Horatius Bonar's hymn, "Thy way, not mine, O L His tune for Psalm 47 is an earlier tune for Samuel Crossman's exqu hymn, "My song is love unknown." His younger brother William was killed while fighting on the Royalist side in the Civil War.

EDMUND SPENSER

PHILIPP NICOLAI
"How brightly shines the morning star!"

In July 1597 plague swept through the small town of Unna in Westpha[l]
where Philipp Nicolai was the Lutheran pastor. In that month alone, 3[0]
people died. It continued to reap havoc through the town until the follow[ing]
January, when cold weather killed off the germs. In those seven months [of]
hell, 1,300 of his parishioners perished.

Nicolai's parsonage overlooked the churchyard, where every time he look[ed]
out of the window he could see the rows of hastily dug new grav[es.]
Sometimes he was officiating at 30 burials in a single day. It would ha[ve]
been so easy in such circumstances for him to lose heart, sink into desp[air]
and even to lose his faith.

In fact he did exactly the opposite. At first he found himself thinking a [lot]
about death, then of God, and finally of eternal life beyond death. He wro[te]
"There seemed to me nothing more sweet, delightful and agreeable, than [the]
contemplation of the noble, sublime doctrine of eternal life, obtained throu[gh]
the blood of Christ. This I allowed to dwell in my heart day and night, a[nd]
searched the Scriptures as to what they revealed on the matter, read also [the]
sweet treatise of the ancient doctor, St. Augustine."

Despite spending hours at the bedsides of dying parishioners, and breathi[ng]
in the air of hovels where whole families were stricken, he found himself

perfect health throughout the ordeal. Just as remarkably he was positively joyous in spirit, so he was able to bring comfort to the grieving families around him.

When it was finally over in January 1598, he wrote: "Now has the gracious, holy God most mercifully preserved me amid the dying from the dreadful pestilence, and wonderfully spared me beyond all my thoughts and hopes, so that with the Prophet David I can say to Him, 'O how great is thy goodness, which thou has laid up for them that fear thee.'"

Philipp Nicolai's experience was remarkably similar to that of Martin Rinkart, featured in Volume 1 of this series. He was the Lutheran pastor at Eilenburg in Saxony some 40 years later, during the Thirty Years' War. His town had a wall round it, which caused country-folk to flock to it for some protection from the looting and indiscriminate killing that was going on in the countryside.

The population swelled to such proportions that plague was inevitable. Over 8,000 of the inhabitants died, and Rinkart buried half of them. This in turn was followed by an appalling famine, and with morale so low, Rinkart wrote his memorable hymn "Now thank we all our God," to remind his flock to count their blessings. At least they were still alive!

About twenty years after this, a Derbyshire clergyman called William Mompesson was faced with the same predicament in his village of Eyam. Out of a population of 330, 259 of his parishioners died from the plague. He visited every stricken dwelling, and imposed a strict quarantine on the village, reminding his flock that if they tried to leave the village they would be messengers of death.

The plague lasted in Eyam for 391 days, yet during the entire time Mompesson himself never had the least sign of illness. He lost his wife Catherine to the pestilence, but it never caused his faith to waver.

Philipp Nicolai's reaction when the plague at Unna was finally over was to write a treatise, which he called 'A Mirror of Joy'. In it he included his two well-known hymns. One of them, "How brightly shines the morning star!"

he had actually written during the days of the plague. It was first publisl
in 1599.

One morning when the plague was at its most rampant he had been pacing
and down his study, trying to shut out for a few minutes the wailing a
death all around him. He then felt an utter calm engulf him, and he was a
to contemplate quite methodically the Saviour's love and the joys t
awaited after death. All this he set down in his hymn.

He became completely absorbed in it, so much so that he forgot all about
mid-day meal. He did not move from his desk until the hymn was fina
completed, by which time the afternoon had almost gone. The second ver
according to the translation by William Mercer, starts:

> "Though circled by the hosts on high,
> He deigns to cast a pitying eye
> Upon his helpless creature:
> The whole creation's Head and Lord,
> By highest seraphim adored,
> Assumes our very nature."

Several translations from the original German have been made, apart fr
this one by Mercer. Among the most popular have been versions
Catherine Winkworth, Frances Elizabeth Cox and R.C. Singleton. The hy
became a great favourite in Germany, and was sung at almost every weddi
It was also frequently chosen for funerals.

The popularity of the hymn was greatly endorsed by the beautiful mel
'Frankfort', sometimes called the 'Queen of Chorales'. It is probably
original tune by Nicolai himself, although he may have had parts sugges
to him by earlier melodies. It is certainly a tune that helps, with the poem
"flood with light earth's darkest places."

The other splendid hymn contained in his work 'A Mirror of Joy' is
thrilling Advent hymn, "Sleepers, wake, a voice is calling." Like "H
brightly shines the morning star!" it has perfect rhymes and another master
melody, again composed by Nicolai himself. It is so good that it was used

Felix Mendelssohn for his oratorio 'St. Paul', and by J.S. Bach in a favourite cantata.

It never really occurred to Philipp Nicolai to be anything other than a Lutheran pastor. He was born in 1556 at Mengeringhausen in Waldeck, where his father Dieterich Nicolai was the pastor. At the age of nineteen he entered the University of Erfurt and the following year transferred to Wittenberg University. He graduated three years later and lived for a while at Volkhardinghausen, close to his parents. In fact he often used to preach for his father.

In 1583, at the age of 27, he was appointed the Lutheran preacher at Herdecke, but it proved a contentious time for young Philipp. The members of the town council were Roman Catholics, and he expressed his Lutheran opposition to their views in no uncertain language. Things came to a head in 1586 when Spanish troops invaded the area, and as a placatory gesture his colleague introduced the Mass. In protest, Philipp resigned his post.

But by now he had made his mark as a forceful preacher and a caring pastor, and he had plenty of support in the area. In 1587 he was appointed pastor at Niederwildungen, near Waldeck, and a year later he was chief pastor at Altwildungen. There he was also court preacher to the widowed Countess Margaretha of Waldeck and tutor to her son, Count Wilhelm Ernst. He died at the age of fourteen, and his death affected Nicolai deeply.

More acrimony followed when his conscience forced him to most ardently support the Lutheran side in what became known as the Sacramentarian controversy, and as a result he was forbidden to preach by Count Franz of Waldeck. But the ban was soon removed as the clergy of Waldeck sided with his Lutheran principles.

In 1596 he became pastor at Unna in Westphalia at the age of 40, and once again he found himself plunged into controversy. This time it was with the Calvinists. But all that became of no importance to anyone when the plague took hold in mid-summer. When that finally took away its last victims in January 1598, a new menace arrived, an invasion of Spanish troops. Nicolai was forced to flee the town, along with other influential Protestants, but they were able to return home the following year.

In 1601, still aged only 45, he was instituted chief pastor at St. Katherine Church in Hamburg, one of the most influential appointments in the city. He became a highly respected figure in Hamburg. He proved himself a popu and powerful preacher, and a pillar of the Lutheran Church in the town. A those who knew him personally found him a most loveable person in I private life. So it comes as something of a surprise to find his writings oft acerbic and sometimes violent in tone. His abiding passion was to conser Lutheranism in its purest doctrines, at whatever cost.

But his time in Hamburg was destined to be short. In 1608 he who h survived a plague with scarcely more than a headache, picked up a fev which caused him to feel unwell. He never recovered from it, and died at t age of 52.

ROBERT ROBINSON
"Come, thou fount of every blessing"

Robert Robinson was born in Norfolk in 1735. His family had to face a constant struggle for subsistence, and as Robert's father died when he was still a young boy, the family was faced with real poverty. Mrs. Robinson's ambition was for her son to become a clergyman, but without an adequate education this seemed a forlorn hope.

Robert was a serious lad who taught himself to read and write from any books that came his way. But he had to make his own way in the world, and this necessitated his removal to London. Far more employment opportunities existed there than among the turnip fields of home. There he was apprenticed to a barber, but he found his days snipping away at the flea and nit-ridden hair of the inhabitants of the metropolis long and tedious.

Young lads cast forth among the temptations of London all too easily found themselves making for the ale-houses when the day's work was done. On one occasion, when Robert was sixteen, he and his companions fell in with an old fortune-teller. As a diversion they set about making her drunk, but she still insisted on attaching herself to Robert and foretelling for him his future life. She told him that he would see not only his children but also his grandchildren, not that common an occurrence in those days of early death in the less fashionable parts of towns. Although his comrades taunted the old lady and plied her with drink, her prediction made Robert think seriously about himself.

Shortly afterwards he attended an open-air meeting addressed by the great itinerant preacher, George Whitefield. He took as his text "The wrath to come," from the 3rd chapter of St. Matthew's Gospel. It was a solemn sermon that cajoled sinners to repent and turn to a life in Christ, and so powerful was the oratory that many who heard it went home in pensive mood. One of these was young Robert.

He did indeed amend his ways and in due course even became a clergyr
But he found it hard to cast off completely his frivolous ways, and throug
his life he suffered from times of guilt, when his old habits of drinking
back-sliding got the better of him.

This he depicts in his most famous hymn, written when he was 23. The
verse illustrates the joy he experienced from the boundless mercy of God:

"Come, thou fount of every blessing,
Tune my heart to sing thy grace:
Streams of mercy, never ceasing,
Call for songs of loudest praise.
Teach me some melodious measure,
Sung by flaming tongues above:
O the vast, the boundless treasure
Of my Lord's unchanging love!"

But, honest man that he was, his own indiscretions haunt him in vers
when he writes:

"Jesus sought me when a stranger,
Wandering from the fold of God;
He, to rescue me from danger,
Interposed his precious blood."

Again in verse 3 he admits his inconstancy when with heartfelt sincerit
pleads:

"Prone to wander, Lord, I feel it;
Prone to leave the God I love:
Take my heart, O take and seal it,
Seal it from thy courts above."

It is a hymn that struck a chord with many generations of church-goers,
in later days was often sung to the tune 'Falfield', composed by Sir Ar
Sullivan. In Robinson's own generation it was set to the melody 'Corir
by Samuel Webbe. In Victorian times the hymn was used by Moody

Sankey in their missions, and was included in their hymnal 'Sacred Songs and Solos'.

It would be good to be able to report that Robert overcame his dependence on the bottle and his more frivolous habits as the years went by, but sadly this does not appear to have been the case. Late in his life he was once travelling by stage coach and entered into conversation with his sole travelling companion. She was a lady, and noting his clerical collar she started talking to him about hymns.

She told him of the immense comfort she had gained from "Come, thou fount of every blessing," entirely unaware that she was addressing the author of her favourite hymn. Robert tried to steer the conversation away from the hymn, but his companion persisted in relating its praises.

Finally, in a state of considerable mental agitation, he could stand it no longer, and confided: "Madam, I am the poor, unhappy man who composed that hymn many years ago; and I would give a thousand worlds, if I had them, to enjoy the feelings I had then!"

Robert Robinson died in 1790, aged 55, a despondent soul who left us a legacy of sincere and poignant sacred verse.

MICHAEL BRUCE
"Where high the heavenly temple stands"

On the opposite shore of Loch Leven to Kinross stands the small village
Kinnesswood, populated by a lot more sheep than people. In a croftea
cottage there in the 18th century, Alexander Bruce struggled to make a livia
for his wife and eight children as a weaver. But the family had one treasua
their fifth child Michael, born in 1746.

Mother and father realised early on that he was a boy of unusual ability, aa
they determined that although they were poor, Michael would have the ba
education that they could manage. Michael loved to be out among the wi
natural environment of his home area, tending the sheep, watching the sun s
over the water of the loch and noting the nests of the birds that graced b
village in such profusion.

Michael's father Alexander was an elder at the independent chapel in t
village, and as is by no means uncommon with those souls who spend a lot
time communing with nature, Michael grew up with a firm faith. At the a
of eleven he resolved to be a minister when he grew up.

Five years later his father received a small bequest, which he decided
devote to Michael's education. He enrolled him in the Greek class
Edinburgh University, where Michael worked with unusual zeal. Only ta
conscious of the sacrifice that his parents were making, he soon expanded b
studies to include Hebrew, natural philosophy and poetry.

It was his poetry studies that were to be his true love. The pensi
melancholy and vivid reaches of imagination so often found in men aa
women of true genius were given free rein by this particular course of stuc
For the rest of his short life, a rhyming couplet was never far from his mind

When he left university he took a post as master of the small school
Gairney Bridge, south of Kinross and today within a stone's throw of t
M90 motorway. He had 28 pupils, each paying two shillings a quarter, w

free board and lodging from their parents in rotation. The children must have been delighted with their new master, who no doubt was eager enough to abandon multiplication tables for the day to go and search with them for the buzzards' nest.

At one of the cottages where he received board and lodging he fell in love with the daughter, who was receiving tuition from Michael in the evenings. She either did not return his affection or was discouraged from doing so by her family, for the affair ended in heartbreak for Michael. But he perpetuated the experience in his poem 'Alexis', rich in the plaintive eloquence of a scholarly lover.

A year later in 1766, perhaps to try and rid his mind of the unsuccessful love affair, he moved south to a school near Alloa. It was there that he wrote his 'Lochleven', a descriptive poem in blank verse.

But his body was by now racked by consumption, and as winter came on he had to abandon all the plans he had made for his life and return home to his parents. These good souls, who had brought him up with such solicitude, became his loving companions in the final months of his life.

His final lines were a celebration of the return of spring in the year 1767, and a sad acceptance that he would never see another one:

> "... but not for me returns
> The vernal joy my better years have known;
> Dim in my breast life's dying taper burns,
> And all the joys of life with health are flown."

Michael was a modest boy throughout his life, naïve in the affairs of the world and seeing only the good side in his fellow humans. He had a warm heart and a wonderful imagination. His death was a sad day for the people of Kinnesswood, many of whom remembered him comparatively recently scampering about among the woods and hills. It was also a sad day for Scottish poetry.

One of the most beautiful of his shorter poems, which displays the joy and innocence of his work, is 'To the Cuckoo'. If he knew about the anti-social habits of this bird, which he surely did, he typically gives them no mention concentrating instead on the more endearing characteristics:

"Hail, beauteous stranger of the wood,
   Attendant on the spring!
Now Heaven repairs thy rural seat,
   And woods thy welcome sing.

Soon as the daisy decks the green
   Thy certain voice we hear;
Hast thou a star to guide thy path
   Or mark the rolling year?

Delightful visitant, with thee
   I hail the time of flowers,
When heaven is filled with music sweet
   Of birds among the bowers.

The schoolboy, wandering in the Wood
   To pull the flowers so gay,
Starts, thy curious voice to hear,
   And imitates thy lay.

Soon as the pea puts on the bloom
   Thou fliest thy vocal vale,
An annual guest in other lands,
   Another spring to hail

Sweet bird, thy bower is ever green,
   Thy sky is ever clear;
Thou hast no sorrow in thy song,
   No winter in thy year!

O could I fly I'd fly with thee!
   We'd make, with social wing,
Our annual visit o'er the globe,
   Companions of the spring

Michael Bruce wrote many of his poems and hymns for the choir a Kinnesswood, who set them to suitable tunes. They were much used and indeed loved by his family and friends, and shortly before he died he copied them out in a quarto manuscript book. No doubt he hoped that one day they would be published, a memorial to his short life.

His friend the Rev'd. John Logan called on his family shortly after Michael' death, requesting permission to borrow the manuscript book so that he could publish the poems. His father Alexander granted the request, but nothing happened for three years. Then a book of poems bearing Michael's name was published, but it did not include the sacred verse, or gospel sonnets as Alexander Bruce called them.

He wrote to Logan, who was then a minister in South Leith, on several occasions asking for the hymns to be returned, but he received no answer to his letters. Finally, Alexander Bruce went to Edinburgh to confront Logan, and demanded the return of the manuscript book. Logan handed over a few scraps of paper but not the book, claiming that the servants had singed fowls with the pages.

Eleven years went by and then Logan published another book of poems, this time in his own name. They included Michael's hymns so familiar to the Kinnesswood choir, who had by no means forgotten their very own poet. Logan hoped that with the passage of time he would get away with stealing Michael's work, and pass it off as his own.

Several hymnals, confused by the whole situation, attributed the hymns to both Bruce and Logan, but they were entirely Bruce's work. It is commensurate with Logan's character that he was eventually forced to resign his pasturate at Leith, or otherwise face deposition.

One of Michael's hymns that Logan claimed as his own is "Where high the heavenly temple stands." In verse 5 we have a glimpse of Michael's staunch faith, that withstood the pain and heartbreak of his unsuccessful fight against consumption:

> "In every pang that rends the heart,
> The Man of Sorrows had a part;
> He sympathises with our grief,
> And to the sufferer sends relief."

Who knows, had he not died at the age of 21 he might have become every bit as famous as Keats, Shelley or Byron, and Scotland would have delighted in another hero called Bruce, to rank beside the great Robert.

WILLIAM BLAKE
"And did those feet in ancient time"

Had anyone asked William Blake his profession, he would probably ha
told them he was an engraver, or possibly an artist. We today would descri
him as an important 18th century poet, renowned to us since our childhood i
such poems as 'The Lamb' or 'The Tiger'. Such verses as:

> "Tiger! Tiger! burning bright
> In the forests of the night,
> What immortal hand or eye
> Could frame thy fearful symmetry?"

from the former poem, or:

> "Little lamb, who made thee?
> Dost thou know who made thee?
> Gave thee life and bid thee feed,
> By the stream and o'er the mead"

from the latter, may well have been committed to memory since schooldays.

He also wrote much longer poems. His work 'Milton' took him four years i
complete, and in the preface to it we find what has become the famous hym
'Jerusalem'. It now has the status almost of a second National Anthem,
regular spot at 'The Last Night of the Proms' and it is an emotion.
experience wherever it is sung. Blake claimed that the poem was dictated i
him by divine powers.

William Blake was born in Golden Square, London, in 1757, the son of
well-to-do hosier. He had no formal education but nevertheless managed i
read and write from his own efforts. His father encouraged his enthusias
for art by buying him casts and giving him generous pocket money from tim
to time.

At the age of ten he was sent along to Par's drawing school in the Strand, where he quickly became an exceptional pupil. The local auctioneer also helped him acquire prints and drawings, knocking down the odd lot rather quicker than he ought to have done to "his little connoisseur" squatting below the hammer. His favourite artists were Raphael, Michael Angelo and Giulio Romano.

He started to write verse at the age of eleven, and from the outset his poems showed a vivid imagination, ignoring realism in favour of an inner world of visionary delights. His father decided that his career should take a more practical turn, so when William was fourteen he apprenticed him to James Basire, the engraver to the Society of Antiquaries.

James Basire was a kind and considerate master, but his engravings were rather flat and mechanical. His drawing, however, was of excellent technique, and this was of undoubted value to William at this stage in his career. In summer Basire sent William off to draw the monuments in Westminster Abbey and other London churches, a task that engrossed him so much that he lost all sense of time and frequently had to be turned out at closing time. In winter he learnt the technique of engraving his drawings.

When his apprenticeship ended after the customary seven years he became for a short time a student at the Royal Academy. Unfortunately he had nothing in common with his master, Moser, who informed him that he should not study the "old, hard, stiff, dry, unfinished" works of art of Raphael and Michael Angelo.

William Blake preferred painting subjects from his own imagination rather than models or set scenes. He had visionary powers and could see the creations of his imagination with amazing clarity. As a boy this had sometimes infuriated his father. On one occasion he returned from a walk and related to his parents how he had seen angels walking about among the hay-makers. His father regarded this fantasy as a deliberate lie and threatened to give young William a good hiding, but fortunately his mother intervened on her son's behalf.

She appreciated that William could see far deeper than the outward appearance of things. Later in life he once said, "I see not with my outward eyes. I see through them and not with them."

A friend once called on him at home and found him engrossed in a portrait, glancing up repeatedly before returning to his pad and drawing busily.

"Disturb me not," he muttered, "I have one sitting to me."

His astonished friend was bemused. "Where is he and what is he? I see no one," remonstrated his friend.

"But I see him, sir," replied Blake. "There he is, his name is Lot. You may read of him in the Scriptures. He is sitting for his portrait."

He felt he had a mission to guide people to a spiritual view of life, and not merely pragmatic interpretation. He wrote: "I have a doctrine to preach. cease not from my great task, to open the immortal eyes of man inward to the eternal worlds."

That was his philosophy, but we must return to William as a young man embarking upon his career. After he finished his studies at the Royal Academy he supported himself mainly by undertaking engraving work for the booksellers. London was an invigorating place for an impressionable young man to inhabit in those days, and in 1780, when he was 23, he was involuntarily involved in the Gordon Riots. He became engulfed in a crowd surging through the streets on their way to storm Newgate Prison, and it must have been a shock to him to witness at first hand the lengths to which desperate men will go.

Two years later he married a lovely girl called Catherine Boucher, who was to prove herself the perfect wife for a visionary man of genius. She put up with long spells of isolation when William was completely engrossed in his work, and periods of real poverty and hardship with never a murmur. On the contrary, she encouraged and supported him with loving devotion, once remarking, "I have very little of Mr. Blake's company. He is always in Paradise!"

Their first home was in Leicester Fields, an area where scrubby farmland stretched right into the heart of town. William was devoted to his young wife, calling her "the sweet shadow of my delight."

Two years after they were married, William exhibited two works at the Royal Academy. In his mid-20s he was starting to earn for himself a reputation as an artist, but his bread and butter was still his engraving work. He opened a print-seller's shop in Broad Street in partnership with a fellow engraver, which struggled along for three years without really earning enough to support them all.

In 1787 sorrow descended on the household with the death of Robert, William's younger brother who lived with them. They were both very fond of Robert, and missed his cheery presence dreadfully. He also used to manage the shop, and his death was a major reason in giving it up.

By now William had completed his important work 'Songs of Innocence', but he could not find a publisher for it. Spurred on by Catherine, who was convinced of its quality, he decided to reproduce it himself. Catherine ventured out with their last half-crown to buy the necessary materials.

The verse was written, the margin decorations were outlined on copper with an impervious liquid and the remainder of the plate eliminated, so that the letters and outlines were left prominent. These could now be printed off in any required tint. William worked up each page by hand with superb detail and variety of illustration. Catherine made herself an expert at the technical work of binding, so the little book was crafted by husband and wife into a creation of real beauty.

In his mid-30s William moved his family to Lambeth. He continued to design and engrave plates for publishers, and as he never liked to turn down work he pushed himself to relentless levels of industry. With his fiery, restless and creative imagination he combined the virtue of extreme patience. Engraving was a tedious task for him, but after it he found the writing and design side of his work mere recreation. When he was advised to take a break from his work he replied, "I don't understand what you mean by my want of a holiday."

But in 1800 they did get away to the seaside, for three years. William took
job offered by a wealthy country squire called Hayley, at Felpham, nea
Bognor Regis, engraving books for his library. Mr. Hayley was a kir
employer and they lived in Rose Cottage, a charming house with a thatche
roof and a lovely country garden.

Unfortunately the work was not as idyllic as its surroundings. Willia
became frustrated at the triviality of his tasks, which had no vent for h
creative genius, and Mr. Hayley's patronage of the arts was shallow ar
sentimental.

The end of their sojourn in rural Sussex was precipitated by a mo
unfortunate incident that affected William deeply. Felpham was considere
to be a likely landing-place for a Napoleonic invasion, and a drunken soldi
who was quartered at the village inn accused William of treason. The soldi
claimed that William had been warning local people that when the Frenc
landed they would either have to join them or have their throats cut.

It was a ridiculous charge without an iota of truth in it, but nevertheless it le
to a trial for treason at Chichester. The case was dismissed with the contem
it deserved, but it caused William a good deal of mental anguish, and it too
him some years to fully recover from it.

They returned to London and in 1808 he exhibited for the last time at tl
Royal Academy. As the years crept on he suffered from ill-health, and wa
no longer able to keep up the frenetic pace of his engraving years. This led
a period of poverty and neglect later in his life, and in 1820 he and Catherir
moved to the Strand, which was then a poor area of town. While there l
engraved the illustrations for 'Inventions to the Book of Job' for Jol
Linnell, a quite masterful work.

William Blake died in 1827 at the age of 70. He said he was going to th
country he had all his life wished to see, and on his death-bed he burst o
into song.

He wrote his great hymn 'Jerusalem' when he was living at Rose Cottag
The first verse was inspired by his creative imagination rather than in a
possible basis in fact.

"And did those feet in ancient time
  Walk upon England's mountains green?
And was the holy Lamb of God
  On England's pleasant pastures seen?
And did the countenance divine
  Shine forth upon our clouded hills?
And was Jerusalem builded here
  Among those dark satanic mills?

Nevertheless it is a lovely image, typical of his inner vision, to picture Jesus walking on English mountains and hills and leading his disciples across green fields under our grey skies.

William lived at the start of the Industrial Revolution, when the green moorlands of the north and midlands were being covered by coalmines, mills, slums and hovels.   Tuberculosis lurked in the alleys, child labour and drunkenness blighted family life and the age was "devoid of sweetness and of light."

The vision of the City of the Lord on English soil, full of happy faces with no want or greed or exploitation was to William Blake a vision of Utopia, even if it was an unattainable dream.

The poem that contained 'Jerusalem' was finished in 1804, but it was not until 1916 that it became a hymn.   In that year Robert Bridges asked Sir Hubert Parry if he could set the verses to a tune that could be used by the Fight for the Right movement at a meeting in Queen's Hall.

Parry came up with his magnificent melody, which was also sung to the words of 'Jerusalem' at a meeting at the Albert Hall to celebrate the suffragettes attaining votes for women.   Since then the hymn has been firmly established as one of the nation's favourites, voted No. 6 by BBC 'Songs of Praise' viewers in January 2005.

Nearly all of William's literary works had this mystical ingredient to them. He detested conventions and codes of morality, preferring to pursue the more exalted paths of love and imagination.   Later on, his work was more

27

preoccupied with the promise of forgiveness of sins through the sacrifice of Christ. His faith was immensely important to him, and caused him to smile his way through the trials and tribulations of life.

THOMAS KELLY
"The head that once was crowned with thorns"

Like William Pennefather but almost half a century before him, Thomas Kelly was born in Dublin in 1769. His father, also called Thomas, was a judge to the Irish Court of Common Pleas. Thomas junior was educated at Trinity College, Dublin, and the family intended him to follow the family tradition and make the law his career. To this end, he moved on to the Temple in London.

Like many a young man of his social standing with Irish blood in him, he enjoyed life to the full, frequenting bars of a different kind to the one intended for him by his father. But his outlook on life was completely changed when he happened by chance to attend a religious revival meeting, where the speaker manifested in him a complete spiritual conversion.

He took Holy Orders for the Church of Ireland in 1792, at the age of 23. Along with his friend Rowland Hill, an Englishman 25 years older than he was and a product of Eton and St. John's College, Cambridge, he started preaching with fervent Evangelical zeal along the Dublin streets and quays. This must have been somewhat embarrassing for his judicial father, and certainly came to the notice of Archbishop Fowler, the Archbishop of Dublin. He decreed their oratory dangerous, and banned both men from preaching in the city.

Undeterred, Kelly took his example from John Bunyan, a man he much admired, who had once been offered his liberty by a judge if he would undertake to stop his preaching. "If you let me out today, I will preach again tomorrow," declared Bunyan and remained in prison. Kelly lived in an age when Nonconformist preachers were no longer imprisoned, so he set up his pulpit in two unconsecrated Dublin chapels, one in Plunket Street and the other the Bethesda.

As his following grew, he seceded from the Established Church of Ireland and set up his own independent chapels in such places as Athy, Portarlington

and Wexford. But he was no irresponsible rabble-rouser. Indeed, he wa
man of considerable scholarship, with a profound knowledge of the Bit
He also acquired linguistic skills in several Oriental languages. He was a
a talented musician, who composed tunes for many of his hymns.
adapted music to every form of metre in his hymn-book, often using obsc
metres that had rarely been tried before.

Always courteous and friendly, he did not court controversy with
Established church, but like the Wesleys, accepted with some sadness
inevitable split because of their differences. Throughout his life he shov
kindness and concern for the poor and destitute, and he was a friend to go
men and women of every creed and at every level of society.

His contemporaries admired his enthusiasm for the Evangelical cause and
eagerness to go out and find lost souls in the streets and alleys rather th
waiting in vain for them to find their way to the churches. Thomas Kell
humility was an example to many clerics in more exalted positions. In
years of famine in Ireland in the 1840s he constantly dug deep into his poc
to provide practical help for those in dire need.

As with that other great Evangelist, Charles Wesley, writing hymns beca
almost an obsession to Kelly. Over a 51 year period he wrote 765 of the
many of them hymns of praise. Those that survive to the present day inclu
"The head that once was crowned with thorns," "The Lord is ris'n indee
"Come, see the place where Jesus lay," "On the mountain's top appeari
and "We sing the praise of him who died."

All Kelly's hymns are of high quality and many first rate ones ha
disappeared from the hymnals. In Victorian times, when so many hymn
were first produced, editors were reluctant to indulge in much origi
research. Instead they relied on those already in publication. The earli
collection of Thomas Kelly's hymns appeared in 1804 under the title 'Hyn
on Various Subjects'. After various other editions, the most comprehens
collection was published in 1853 in both London and Dublin, under
simple title 'Hymns'.

"The head that once was crowned with thorns" is an Ascension-tide hy
that first appeared in 1820. It is a Christian cry of joy, confident in

certain victory over sin and death won for us by Our Lord on the cross. The words are clearly the words of a scholar and a poet, and the tune 'St. Magnus' complements it beautifully, being full of exultation. Its likely composer was Jeremiah Clarke, organist of Winchester Cathedral and then St. Paul's Cathedral in the late 17th century.

His death at the age of 37 casts a shadow over the singing of this glorious hymn of praise and adoration. Clarke had been jilted by the lady he was very much in love with, and in a fit of deep depression he determined to take his own life. The only question was whether to shoot or drown himself. He decided to toss a coin, but it fell on its edge in the mud beside a pond. Instead of interpreting this as a sign that he should do neither, he returned to his home close to St. Paul's and shot himself.

Thomas Kelly continued writing his hymns and preaching with characteristic fervour until he was barely able to climb the steps to the pulpit. He died in 1854 at the age of 85.

HENRY KIRKE WHITE
"Oft in danger, oft in woe"

Henry Kirke White was born in Nottingham in 1785. His father was a po
butcher, and for much of his life Henry had to deliver the leaky packages
meat around the neighbourhood. But he had a brilliant mind, and aspired tc
literary career. Regrettably he never achieved this, for he died when he w
21. Had he lived, he might well have been bracketed with Byron, Keats a
Shelley as one of the great poets of his age.

His mother, Mary, came from a Staffordshire family of some note, and wa:
woman of considerable learning. It was she who gave Henry his ea
education, and his quest for learning was unquenchable. At the age of sev
he was an avid reader of everything that came his way, from the books in l
mother's closet to the newspaper that the meat was wrapped in.

It was not long before he was writing poetry, and sketches of life
Nottingham. This did not please his father John, who considered that l
son's career should be as his assistant in the butchery trade. Henry had
aversion to the pathetic carcasses of animals hanging from hooks in t
scullery, the stench of animal blood and the slaughter that sometimes went
in their own back yard.

By the time he was thirteen Henry was writing poetry of true worth. He h
also taught himself to speak French, and was as forward with his studies a:
bright student who had spent years at grammar school. But his father forc
him to spend most of the day trudging round the back streets of the town w
his butcher's basket.

Study was allowed after the shop closed for the day, but a year later his fat
forbade even this, in the hope that Henry would devote more of his energ
to the trade which he detested so bitterly. But his mother came to the resc
She started a boarding and day school for girls, presumably in premises

enough removed from home that the girls were saved from the sounds of the squealing piglets and the butcher's chopper thumping against the hornbeam block.

The added income to the family budget was enough to persuade John White to release his son from the butcher's basket, and instead he was apprenticed to an attorney. But the family could not afford the initial premium, which increased Henry's period of servitude.

His office duties do not appear to have been too arduous, however, for sitting at his high stool he found time to teach himself Latin, make marked progress in Greek and add Italian, Spanish and Portuguese to his linguistic accomplishments. Perhaps his employer encouraged this rare talent for learning, for the wills and affidavits seem to have been dispatched with remarkable speed.

Henry also managed to find time to study chemistry, astrology and electricity, and in his precious moments of leisure he found music and drawing engrossing pastimes.

When he was still fourteen he became a regular contributor to some of the periodicals which were then so profuse, particularly the 'Monthly Mirror'. Its editor, Thomas Hill, persuaded him to prepare a volume of poems for publication. It was not a financial success but it did introduce his name to the literary world.

One important figure to take notice of the young poet through the publication of this volume was Robert Southey, who was most enthusiastic in his acclaim. Indeed, Southey later became Henry's biographer, and did much to introduce his name to a wider public.

At this stage of his adolescence Henry wavered on the borderline of scepticism in religious matters, but he experienced a complete conversion and became a deeply committed Christian. He now aimed to preach the faith which only a year previously he had despised.

One of his acquaintances was a Mr. Simeon, who was instrumental in arranging for him a sizarship at St. John's College, Cambridge. This was an early form of bursarship, available at Cambridge and Dublin, that provided

St. JOHN's COLLEGE, CAMBRIDGE, where Henry Kirke
White spent the last years of his short life

impecunious students with an allowance to help with expenses, in return for certain menial duties. Henry worked with such diligence in his first term that at the end of it he was proclaimed the first student in his year.

His ambition now was to win a university scholarship, and he studied with relentless ardour. Everyone considered it a foregone conclusion that this remarkably talented young man would prevail at the forthcoming exam. But long nights of study combined with far too little nutritional food and no healthy exercise proved his undoing. He was so weak when the day of the exam came that he was forced to take to his bed.

Henry never really recovered his health, although he did manage one visit to London, the excitement of which enthused him to rally for a while. He returned to Cambridge the following year, and again attained first place in his year. Both professors and fellow students acknowledged his genius in unstinting praise, and he was to enjoy one more vacation before returning to his college only to die. Poor Henry was only 21.

Perhaps he would have ranked with the great poets of his generation had he lived longer. Shelley and Byron rated him an equal, and it was Byron who wrote of him in the following stanza:

> "Unhappy White, while life was in its spring,
> And thy young muse just waved her joyous wing,
> The spoiler came, and all her boasted care
> Has sought the grave, to sleep for ever there."

Henry Kirke White wrote half a hymn, but it is a good one and is still very popular today. The origin of "Oft in danger, oft in woe" is an intriguing story. It is normally attributed to "Henry Kirke White and Others", and the original version was written by Henry on the back of a Maths exam. He finished the paper early, and as the students were confined to the examination hall until the allotted time was up, he used the time to write the first ten lines of the hymn.

Whether he had found the paper horribly taxing, which seems unlikely in view of his outstanding intellect, or whether he was just feeling depressed is a matter for conjecture. At any rate, his first verse was extremely mournful:

"Much in sorrow, oft in woe,
Onward, Christians, onward go,

Fight the fight, and, worn with strife,
Steep with tears the bread of life."

By a remarkable coincidence, sixteen years later the exam script came into
the possession of Mrs. Fuller-Maitland, who was in the process of compiling
a hymn-book. She could not use an unfinished hymn in her hymnal, but she
showed the script to her fourteen-year-old daughter Frances, who took it up
to her room.

Some time later she emerged, brandishing fourteen additional lines of her
own which completed the hymn. Her extra verses were so good that Mrs.
Fuller-Maitland used the entire hymn in her new book.

Henry's title for the hymn was 'The Christian Soldier Encouraged', but there
is far more encouragement in the lines of Frances than in the morose
beginning written by Henry. The third verse, written by Frances, is
brimming with self-confidence:

"Let your drooping hearts be glad;
March in heavenly armour clad;
Fight, nor think the battle long,
Victory soon shall tune your song."

Henry's first verse was soon amended to the familiar words of today:

"Oft in danger, oft in woe,
Onward, Christians, onward go;
Bear the toil, maintain the strife,
Strengthened with the bread of life."

The tune that the hymn is usually sung to is a positive, confident tune, almost
a marching rhythm, very suitable for Christian soldiers moving onwards. It is
called 'University College' and it was composed by Henry John Gauntlett
He was born in 1805, a year before Henry Kirke White died. He wrote a
number of other well known hymn tunes as well.

WILLIAM BULLOCK
"We love the place, O God"

Whenever a new church or cathedral is consecrated, one of the hymns that is most likely to be chosen for that memorable occasion is "We love the place, O God." It is a particularly appropriate hymn for such an occasion, the first two verses reading:

> "We love the place, O God,
> Wherein thine honour dwells;
> The joy of thine abode
> All earthly joy excels.
>
> We love the house of prayer,
> Wherein thy servants meet;
> And thou, O Lord, art there
> Thy chosen flock to greet."

One can picture the scene. Bishops and clergy are attired in fine vestments, the mayor and local dignitaries are present and a full congregation has assembled for this historic occasion. Craftsmen have pooled their skills in a common purpose of making God's house an abode of majesty and splendour.

But when this hymn was sung for the first time the surroundings were very different. The author of the hymn, William Bullock, was a young naval officer who was attached to a survey expedition along the coasts of Newfoundland. As well as making maps, charting and sounding the depths along the coast, William was also observing the plight of the people who lived there.

He was appalled at their primitive way of life. Poverty was only too apparent in every cove, along with a lack of education and medical facilities. The area was completely cut off from the rest of the world, and what horrified him most of all was an absence of any religious worship or instruction. Bullock determined to do something about it.

He resigned his commission, thereby abandoning a most promising career in the navy, and applied for ordination. He then returned to the storm-battered coasts of Newfoundland as a missionary with the Society for the Propagation of the Gospel, for whom he worked for 32 years.

At an inlet named Trinity Bay he gathered together a small band of Christians, and working when the day's work was done they built a small church out of wood. It was primitive, draughty and unpretentious, but it was a labour of love. And for its consecration, William wrote his famous hymn.

He included an additional verse which was omitted by Sir Henry Williams Baker when he edited the hymn for inclusion in 'Hymns Ancient and Modern'. It was:

> "We love thy saints, who come
> Thy mercy to proclaim,
> To call the wanderers home,
> And magnify thy name."

This verse was intended to refer to the preachers who proclaimed the faith from the pulpit of the tiny church.

The tune 'Quam dilecta' is the work of a 19th century composer, Bishop Henry Jenner, one time Bishop of Dunedin. It is simple, quiet and sincere and seems to be universally used for the hymn. Although Bullock's hymn was written for a church consecration service, it can be sung at any time of the Christian year, and several hymnals include it in their 'General Hymns' section.

William's ministry in the northern wastes of Canada flourished, and he was eventually appointed Dean of Halifax, Nova Scotia. This was a veritable Mecca of civilisation after some of the conditions he had endured in Newfoundland. He died in 1874, having dedicated his life to bringing souls to Christ in foreign climes.

He left behind him two works. One was his 'Songs of the Church', his own hymnal printed in 1854 at his own expense. The hymns in it were "written amidst the various scenes of missionary life," he wrote, "and are intended for

38

the private and domestic use of Christians in new countries deprived of all public worship." He also wrote an earlier work, 'Practical Lectures upon the History of Joseph and his Brethren', published in 1826.

JOHN HAMPDEN GURNEY
"Ye holy angels bright"

John Hampden Gurney was born near London's Fleet Street in 1802. His father was a judge, rather a severe one by all accounts and one hopes for the sake of the family that he saved his severity for the courtroom. The Establishment thought highly of him, for he was knighted for his services to justice.

Young John was educated at Trinity College, Cambridge, where so many eminent theologians and writers in the past had learnt their art. He started to study law, but changed to theology which was far more to his liking. At the age of 25 he was ordained by the Bishop of Lincoln.

His first post was as assistant curate at Lutterworth, a pleasant Leicestershire market town that was the home of John Wycliffe, who sowed the seed for the Reformation almost 500 years previously. Gurney remained at Lutterworth for twenty years, and it seems odd that the judge did not buy him an incumbency of his own.

In 1847 Gurney was appointed by the Crown to be rector of the fashionable St. Mary's, Bryanston Square in Marylebone, where he remained until his death fifteen years later. He quickly gained a reputation as a most popular and forceful preacher, which resulted in his appointment to a prebendary stall at St. Paul's Cathedral.

When he was at Lutterworth he married Mary, a minister's daughter from Edinburgh. He was also chaplain to the Poor Law Union in Lutterworth, but when not out and about the town on his parochial duties he would be at home in his study. There his desk would be covered with books, letters, half written poems and reams of paper, for his abiding interest was in hymns and the compilation of hymnals.

He published two of these, along with numerous sermons, historical pieces on such events as the Indian Mutiny and the death of Wellington, and a collection of the talks that he gave to the YMCA.

His hymn "We saw thee not when thou didst come" was inspired by a hymn in a small American volume which Gurney described as "well conceived but very imperfectly executed." Working independently to Gurney, the Misses Carus-Wilson must have come across the same imperfect American hymn, for in 1834 they published their own amendment of it. The first verse goes:

"We have not seen thy footsteps tread
This wild and sinful earth of ours,
Nor heard thy voice restore the dead
Again to life's reviving powers;
But we believe – for all things are
The gifts of thine almighty care."

Four years later John Gurney, then working as a curate at Lutterworth, published his 'Collection of Hymns for Public Worship'. This also included an adaptation of the American hymn, and his first verse read:

"We saw thee not when thou didst tread
In mortal guise this sinful earth,
Nor heard thy voice restore the dead,
And wake them to a second birth;
But we believe that thou didst come,
And leave for us thy glorious home."

Thirteen years later, when he was rector of St. Mary's, Bryanston Square, Gurney republished the hymn in the form that was then used universally. The fourth verse in that version is remarkably similar to that produced by the Misses Carus-Wilson, so it is probable that some cribbing went on.

In a note appearing in his 'Marylebone Hymn Book', Gurney stated that "nothing of the original composition remains, but the first four words and the repeated words." This limits the surviving American version to a mere six words, "We saw thee not" and "We believe."

Another of John Gurney's hymns is "Fair waved the golden corn." The arable harvests in Leicestershire in the mid-19th century must have been very special, for Gurney was gazing out of his study window writing about the golden corn around Lutterworth while Henry Alford was noting that:

> "All is safely gathered in,
> ere the winter storms begin"

from his vicarage at Wymeswold. The two men were contemporaries, and it would be interesting to know whether they ever met up to discuss their interest in hymnody.

The most famous of John Gurney's hymns is another one that was inspired by an earlier hymn. In 1838, the year he produced his 'Hymns for Public Worship' at Lutterworth, Gurney adapted "Ye holy angels bright" in the form that we sing it today for inclusion in his hymnal. He based the hymn on a sacred poem by Richard Baxter, a Puritan from Shropshire who lived in the 17th century.

Although Baxter started his ministry as a Church of England clergyman, he developed a strong distrust of the Established church and bishops. He sided with the Roundheads in the Civil War, and became one of Oliver Cromwell's chaplains. At the Restoration of the Monarchy in 1660 he became chaplain to Charles 11, who offered him the bishopric of Hereford.

Courageously he refused to accept it, left the Church of England when the Act of Uniformity was passed and became a Nonconformist minister. He was tried for sedition before the infamous Judge Jeffreys and was imprisoned for eighteen months. But Gurney provided his memorial with his 19[t] century adaptation of his original very long sacred poem.

The tune that we all enjoy singing "Ye holy angels bright" to is Darwall' 148th by John Darwall, who lived in the 18th century. He was vicar of Walsall, and judging by the way this tune races up and down the scales, he must have kept his choir very much on its toes.

They had plenty of scope for their Sunday worship, for he composed tunes for every one of the 150 psalms. This particular tune he wrote for Psalm 148

42

For us non-choristers who wrestle with the exciting tune today, there is every need to:

"Assist our song,
or else the theme
too high doth seem
for mortal song."

JOHN CHANDLER
"Christ is our corner-stone"

Village clergymen in the 19th century could be roughly divided into fou groups. There were those who loved scholarship and wished to prolong the academic studies in the peace of their vicarage studies. Others entered s fully into the lives of their parishioners that even in a village of only 10 souls, they would be exhausted and spent by their late 50s. A third grou would be conscientious and hard-working clerics, at the same time enjoyin their privileged place in Victorian society. Finally there were those wh wished to live the lives of country gentlemen and enjoy their sportin pursuits, but who had no real call to the ministry.

John Chandler would very definitely fall into the first group. He loved t study the Latin texts of the great ecclesiastical writers from past centurie and to translate some of them into English. His 'Prayers and Meditatior from the Writings of the Divines of the Anglican Church' was very high acclaimed and led to his interest in hymnology.

Another very carefully researched work was his 'Life of William c Wykeham', a man who was born in 1324 in a peasant's cottage at Wickham near Fareham. He was fortunate enough to catch the eye of his local lord c the manor, Nicholas Uvedale, who enrolled him in the grammar school a Winchester. There he learnt mathematics, law and languages as well as th Classics, which no doubt helped him when he became Chancellor of Englan and Bishop of Winchester. For some years under Edward 111 he wa virtually in control of the affairs of the nation. He transformed Wincheste Cathedral, built the College and New College, Oxford, and supervised all th royal castles in the land. John Chandler had a lot to research!

John Chandler wanted to find hymns in his searches of ancient documen that would correspond to the old prayers of the Anglican liturgy. H translated many from their original Latin, including "Christ is our corne stone," "Conquering kings their titles take," "On Jordan's bank the Baptist cry" and "Jesus, our hope, our hearts' desire."

Most of his translations were from the 'Parisian Breviary' and an old book of Latin hymns compiled by Georgius Cassander, printed in Cologne in 1556. He must have spent hours browsing round the antiquarian bookshops in places like Winchester and Guildford, and also London which was accessible from his Surrey home when the railway was opened during his most active years.

20 or 30 of his translations were to be found in hymnals early in the 20th century, and some survive to this day. 'Complete Anglican Hymns Old and New' still retains four of them. His translations were very popular with all Christian sects, although they were considered rather free. He also went to considerable lengths to avoid any sentiments that could be construed as theologically controversial.

"Christ is our corner-stone" is a translation from the Latin of the 7th or 8th centuries and is based on the 2nd chapter of St. Paul's Epistle to the Ephesians, verses 20 – 22. The 'Church Hymnal for the Christian Year' lists it under the heading "Foundation and Consecration of a Church," but it is also a fervent hymn of praise. The first verse abounds with Christian hope and confidence:

> "Christ is our corner-stone,
> On him alone we build;
> With his true saints alone
> The courts of heaven are filled;
> On his great love
> Our hopes we place
> Of present grace
> And joys above."

The most popular tune for this hymn is probably 'Harewood', by Samuel Sebastian Wesley, an almost exact contemporary of the author. It is a pleasing melody, free from any great excesses of musical grandeur. It can also be sung to the tune 'Darwall' by the Rev'd. J. Darwall, or to 'St. Godric', composed by that prolific writer of hymn tunes, the Rev'd. J.B. Dykes.

John Chandler was born at Witley, near Godalming, in 1806. Witley is on
of the most attractive villages in Surrey, and it certainly exuded its charms c
Chandler, who spent most of his life there. The woods around the villag
were ideal for a morning ramble while mulling over his next Sunday sermo
at the same time noting the activities of the greater spotted woodpecker or th
latest badger sett.

The church is full of atmosphere, parts of it dating back to Norman times. I
singular tower, supporting within its parapet a shingled spire, commands
Christian presence that stands sentinel over the villagers as they go abo
their day-to-day work. John Chandler would have known every stone of
for from an early age he listened to his father preaching from the pulpit whic
he in turn was eventually to occupy.

He received most of his Classical education at Corpus Christi Colleg
Oxford, graduating in 1827. Four years later he was ordained, and succeede
his father as vicar of Witley. It must have been odd at first, preaching to th
same folk whom he had played conkers with in his boyhood, and perhaps th
same girls who had smiled at him over the vicarage gate during the colleg
vacations.

George Eliot wrote her last novel, 'Daniel Deronda', at Witley, completing
in 1876. This was the year of Chandler's death, but by then he was living
Putney.

HARRIET MARTINEAU
"All men are equal in their birth"

Harriet Martineau was born in Norwich in 1802. Her father was a stern Unitarian who made his living by manufacturing cloth and fabric. Both parents were well-meaning, but too hidebound by Puritanical beliefs, so home for the children was never a particularly happy place.

Her mother, practical to the point of pedantry, insisted she should drink a pint of milk every day, and in so doing condemned Harriet to an early life of indigestion and bilious attacks. She was educated at home until she was eleven, learning Latin from her older brother Thomas.

She read 'Paradise Lost' when she was seven, and came to know it almost by heart. Later she attended a school in Norwich. Her upbringing, with its emphasis on social and moral correctness, caused her to become something of an introvert as a girl, which was contrary to her natural disposition.

Harriet was at this stage very religious in a strictly practical manner. As Norman Nicholson once memorably described her, "She looked on God, from childhood, as a schoolmaster giving instruction and correcting homework, and later, when she believed that she had learnt the rules, she was quite ready to manage her curriculum without Him!"

She also had to contend with ill health and disabilities from a young age. Harriet never had much sense of taste or smell, which might have been an advantage to her cook in later life but not to her proliferation of house guests. More seriously, by the time she was sixteen she was almost completely deaf, and went around with an enormous ear trumpet into which the people she conversed with were invited to bellow.

Harriet was one of eight children in a home where money was tight, and the family finances reached something of a crisis when her father died in 1826. Harriet was then 24. To make matters worse, the family investments collapsed. Ever the pragmatist, Harriet sat down to work out how she could earn her living and help to support those of the family who still remained at home.

She decided that she could sew, embroider and write, so she set up business to exploit these skills. There was a constant demand for sewi[ng] from the ladies of the cathedral city, and she made little bags and baskets th[at] were bought by the tourists who came to Norwich. But her heart was real[ly] in her writing.

As a girl she had entered a three-fold essay competition, aimed at converti[ng] Roman Catholics, Muslims and Jews to the Protestant faith, and h[er] anonymous entries won each section in turn. She now started writing rath[er] serious stories with a strong religious and moral tone, which she sold to t[he] weekly religious periodicals. Her first article she sold to the 'Month[ly] Repository' when she was nineteen.

The first piece to come to the attention of the critics was an article whi[ch] argued that women had equal capabilities with men for positions [of] leadership, for all her life she was an ardent feminist. The only trouble w[as] that she had no hope of getting it published unless she gave it a ma[le] pseudonym, which she did! The three Bronte sisters had the same dilem[ma] when they sent their first novels off to a publisher.

On the completion of 'Deerbrook', her first novel, she set out for London a[nd] trudged through the streets visiting one publisher's office after another. W[ith] her distinct limp and vast ear trumpet she must have been viewed by t[he] bewhiskered gentlemen behind their desks with a mixture of alarm a[nd] amusement.

But she was so zealous over her mission that one firm, Charles Fox, w[as] finally persuaded to read it through. The proprietor agreed to publish it o[n a] 50 – 50 basis, half of any profits to go to the publishing house and half to h[er.] It was an excellent piece of business on behalf of the publisher, for the fi[rst] edition of 1,500 copies was sold out within ten days.

The book that really caused Harriet Martineau's name to be respected in t[he] literary world was her 'Illustrations of Political Economy', published in 18[30] when she was 30. It was an amazing success for the young author. [It] combined the principles of Adam Smith, Malthus and Ricardo, advocati[ng] the freedom of industry and commerce between nations.

With Malthus she argued that the population of the human race must be in proportion to the amount of food which it could produce. Rather than suggesting that every energy should be thrown into increasing productivity, it tended to suggest that population should be curtailed, in order that it should not overtake food production.

The form of the book was a collection of highly moral stories demonstrating economic truths, designed to be read by all classes of society. In an age when morality was expected and the written word was hungrily devoured by a populace that had no visual media for its mass entertainment, it struck just the right note. Even the King of France sung its praises, until he was informed that the author held dangerous beliefs – she believed in democracy!

In America Harriet Martineau was all the rage, a name to be praised in the drawing-room circles of Boston and the exotic mansions of the deep South, until word filtered through that their heroine supported Negro slaves as well as the republicans in France. Harriet was not aiming to stir up the blood and thunder of a revolution but she was a radical, and sharing her idealism were like-minded literary free-thinkers – Wordsworth, Coleridge, Byron and Shelley.

It is taking something of a liberty to include Harriet in a volume devoted to hymns and hymn-writers, for the intensity of her religious observance waxed and waned at different periods in her life. Her hymns were written in her Unitarian period in her late 20s and early 30s, and were edited by her brother James, who was also a hymn-writer.

Five of them appeared in 'A Collection of Hymns for Christian Worship', which he published for his congregation at Eustace Street Chapel in Dublin. "All men are equal in their birth" was one of them, a hymn on human equality which was typical of Harriet's progressive views on life.

Harriet's life and the career that she had chosen for herself were progressing very positively when suddenly, at the age of 37, she suffered a complete breakdown in her health while travelling on the Continent. For the next five years she suffered continuous pain, sickness and exhaustion. Doctors led her to believe that her condition was incurable, and she convinced herself that this was so.

HARRIET MARTINEAU

For a short time she went to live with one of her sisters in Newcastle, for her brother-in-law was a medical man. So as not to be a burden on the family she then moved to lodgings in Tynemouth. There she strove to keep abreast of her writing and her weighty correspondence, but it was all too much for her.

She found the environment depressing, for the grey stone wall of the harbour, the relentless waves from the North Sea and the bleak moors around the town were a constant dampener on the spirits of the invalid. Just as her life was as black as it could possibly be, there occurred a remarkable transformation. Harriet happened to try mesmerism, and it worked for her in a miraculous way. The invalid who seldom left her room was suddenly tramping the moors, pounding the coastal paths before breakfast, plunging into the North Sea and revelling in the rain, wind and snow. There she was at the age of 42 showing the vitality of a teenager.

Whether her cure was an enormous effort of mind which banished physical disabilities is impossible to say. But at all events, her life took on a new impetus. She finished with landladies, sisters and brothers-in-law, polished floors, physicians and swallowing pills and took on an enthusiasm for starting life all over again.

In her 'Autobiography' she wrote: "My life began with winter. There followed a season of storm and sunshine, merging into a long gloom. But the spring, summer and autumn of life were yet to come." She decided to make a break from Tynemouth with its depressing memories and to seek out a new landscape in keeping with her new life.

She was used to the North by now, with its friendly folk and wild countryside, for she had finished with the flat acres of East Anglia for ever. The Lake District beckoned on the other side of the country, and she decided upon Ambleside for her new home. The year was 1844, the Industrial Revolution was in full swing as she crossed the Pennines, and at the age of 43 her mind was seething with notions that she wanted to write about.

First she needed to acquire a home. She walked out of Ambleside on the Rydal road, past a bridge house built on a circular arch that spans a rushing stream. It is a tiny building, consisting of one room down and the other up, linked by an outside staircase. Almost 400 years ago it was the summerhouse of Ambleside Hall.

A couple of hundred yards past it she came upon the site whereon she determined to build her house – The Knoll. She designed and built the new house herself and fenced in the two acres of land that went with it. Her plan was to start a small dairy herd, using half the acreage that the local farmers advised. Nevertheless, the cows flourished under the care of a dairyman specially brought with her from Norfolk.

Harriet had decided upon a complete life change which even involved abandoning the formal religion of her earlier years. She now declared herself to be an agnostic. She also abandoned the solitary habits of the past, gathering around her in her new home nieces, house guests and resident maids.

The gentry of the district were suspicious of this radical firebrand who had arrived among them. Most ignored her, but her warm and ebullient personality won her friends in the town, for she entered into the life of the community with a cheery enthusiasm. They appreciated her, as was shown by numerous shy little acts. On one occasion, when she needed turf for her new lawn, a pile of neatly cut sods mysteriously appeared in the garden over night.

Just up the road at Rydal Mount in Grasmere, William Wordsworth was a neighbour who did call on several occasions. As he grew older he lost all the radical idealism of his youth and took on the political opinions of a Tory squire, so Harriet would not have had much in common with him. It must also have been difficult for the pair to communicate, for Wordsworth was losing all his teeth so must have found it difficult to enunciate, and Harriet relied on her ear trumpet in order to hear anything.

The Poet Laureate planted a tree in her new garden, dusted off his hands and then clasped hers between both of his. In this earnest posture he tried to give her advice on how to cope with the prying tourists who came every summer to gape at celebrities. Harriet recorded the incident in her 'Autobiography':

" 'When you have a visitor,' he said, 'you must do as we did – you must say, "If you like to have a cup of tea with us, you are very welcome: but if you want any meat, you must pay for your board." Now, promise me that you will do this.' I could promise nothing of the sort. I told him I had rather not invite my friends unless I could make them comfortable."

Harriet was less tolerant with strangers who came to invade her privacy, and for a couple of months at the height of the tourist season each year, she left Ambleside for quieter climes.

One of the tasks she set her builder was to dig a pit in the corner of her garden, near the town Methodist Chapel. It looked rather like a big grave or a small swimming-pool. But in fact she allowed it to fill up with rain water and then used it as a bath, plunging in naked when neighbours and townsfolk were still fast asleep. She would then go for a seven or eight mile walk and come back to breakfast.

Harriet Martineau considered it her duty to attend to the education of Ambleside. The village children were instructed on various topics, and the working population was treated to a series of lectures on English history, America, the Crimean War and sanitation. When she moved on to the dangers of alcohol, her diagrams of the decay of the lining of the stomach were so lurid that one local fellow, notorious for his fondness of the bottle, hurried outside to be sick.

She also founded a building society to illustrate the prudence of saving, built cottages for young local couples, lent books from her library and invited the old men up to her kitchen for their Christmas party.

Harriet possessed the habit of saying exactly what she thought, and as her beliefs tended to be years ahead of her time, this caused some people to distrust her. But the ordinary folk had a great regard for her, and put up with her eccentric habits with an amused benevolence. She was the kindest of neighbours, and although her friends were often startled by her frank, even outrageous views, they accepted that she spoke and wrote from the heart, without malice or any intentional hurt.

Visitors came frequently to The Knoll. The Wordsworths often took the short trip down from Grasmere, and others to bellow into the famous ear-trumpet included George Eliot, Emerson and Elizabeth Gaskell. Catherine Winkworth, who translated much fine German poetry into eloquent English, came up from Manchester. There she attended the same Unitarian church as Harriet's brother, Dr. James Martineau. He was Professor of Mental and Moral Philosophy at Manchester New College.

Hallam, Sydney Smith, Carlyle and Henry Hart Milman also at various times occupied the spare room at The Knoll. Milman was the Dean of St. Paul's, who wrote the hymn 'Ride on, ride on in majesty!' Another visitor, probably introduced by her friend Elizabeth Gaskell, was Charlotte Bronte. She came not long after the rapid deaths of her brother Branwell and sisters Emily and Ann, all within a few months of each other, so she was feeling bereft and despondent.

But she clearly enjoyed her trip to Ambleside, and during the visit wrote about it to her friend Ellen Nussey, a letter which is quoted by Elizabeth Gaskell in her 'Life of Charlotte Bronte'. She gives so much information about Harriet's lifestyle that it is worth quoting from the letter at length:

"I can write to you now, dear E___, for I am away from home, and relieved, temporarily, at least, by change of air and scene, from the heavy depression which, I confess, has for nearly three months been sinking me to the earth. I never shall forget last autumn! Some days and nights have been cruel; but now, having once told you this, I need say no more on the subject. My loathing of solitude grew extreme; my recollection of my sisters intolerably poignant. I am better now. I am at Miss Martineau's for a week. Her house is very pleasant, both within and without; arranged at all points with admirable neatness and comfort. Her visitors enjoy the most perfect liberty; what she claims for herself she allows them. I rise at my own hour, breakfast alone (she is up at five, takes a cold bath, and a walk by starlight, and has finished breakfast and got to her work by seven o'clock). I pass the morning in the drawing-room – she in her study.

At two o'clock we meet – work, talk and walk together, till five, her dinner hour, spend the evening together, when she converses fluently and abundantly, and with the most complete frankness. I go to my own room soon after ten, she sits up writing letters till twelve. She appears exhaustless in strength and spirits, and indefatigable in the faculty of labour. She is a great and good woman; of course not without peculiarities, but I have seen none as yet that annoy me. She is both hard and warm-hearted, abrupt and affectionate, liberal and despotic. I believe she is not at all conscious of her own absolutism. When I tell her of it, she denies the charge warmly; then I laugh at her. I believe she almost rules Ambleside. Some of the gentry dislike her, but the lower orders have a great regard for her... I have truly enjoyed my visit here. I have seen a good many people, and all have been so marvellously kind; not the least so, the family of Dr. Arnold. Miss Martineau I relish inexpressibly."

Harriet's writing was often philosophical in tone. Her critics claimed that it lacked deep research or originality of conception, which was undoubtedly true partly because she worked at such a frenetic pace. She also wrote on a range of social topics, sometimes exposing the wrongs of a greedy and class-divisive age. The public loved her work, and she became one of the most talked about literary figures, although she had to endure those dark years before achieving such eminence.

Her work schedule was a harrowing one. She wrote 1,600 articles for the 'Daily News', more for 'Once a Week' and countless books and pamphlets. Her articles were on almost every subject that caught the interest of that section of the public with progressive views. The American Civil War, India, the Lancashire cotton industry, slavery, slums and sewage systems were all scrutinised with her pragmatic, unsentimental approach. Tens of thousands of people shaped their own opinions from what she wrote in her study at Ambleside.

Lord Brougham, the Chancellor, asked her to write a novel about pauperism, which was duly published under the title 'The Parish'. She was invited to visit America and write for the anti-slavery cause. Harriet had the journalist's gift of turning every new experience, however small, into intriguing copy, full of common sense and sparkle despite the serious message she may be imparting. Three Prime Ministers offered her a civil pension, but not wishing to jeopardise her independence, she refused each one.

She came to know the Lake District very well, and after living there for ten years and travelling around it in a carriage with a friend for research purposes, she published her 'Complete Guide to the Lakes' in 1855. Norman Nicholson, the 20th century poet and writer, who spent all his life in the same terrace house in Millom, acknowledges it as a fair description of the physical geography of the area, but states that she had discovered very little of the character of the place.

Nevertheless, it is a very readable book because she digresses into her own experiences of visiting some of the remoter parts, and we learn of 19th century social and economic issues. For instance, she tells us that Mardale sent 3,000 pounds of butter to Manchester every week. The carrier's cart used to pick up the baskets from the scattered dwellings in the dale and take them to the railway.

Harriet disagreed with Wordsworth, who looked upon the Lake District as an outstanding area of picturesque scenery that must not be spoilt in any way. She rightly believed that the people of the Lake District must join the industrial society of the rest of Britain, demand proper communication routes and seek new trades and industries in the towns and villages. To live in the age old manner in an area of outstanding natural beauty she knew would be disastrous.

She wanted The Lakes to contribute to the economy of the realm, and opposed Wordsworth and his friends who wanted to keep railways away from the region. Already by the mid 19th century the Lake District was showing serious signs of decline. Cottages were crumbling, fields were being left untilled and the young were leaving the rural towns and villages in search of realistic wages in the new industrial towns of Lancashire and Yorkshire.

This is what she had to say in her book about the benefits of the railway:

"We have no fear of injury, moral or economical, from the great recent change, - the introduction of railways. The morals of rural districts are usually such as cannot well be made worse by any change. Drinking and kindred vices abound wherever, in our day, intellectual resources are absent: and nowhere is drunkenness a more prevalent and desperate curse than in

the Lake District. Any infusion of the intelligence and varied interests of the towns-people must, it appears, be eminently beneficial; and the order of work-people brought by the railways is of a desirable kind. And, as to the economical effect, - it cannot but be good, considering that mental stimulus and improved education are above every thing wanted...

In a generation or two the dale-farms may yield wool that Yorkshire and Lancashire, and perhaps other countries may compete for; the cheese may find a market, and the butter may be in request. And at the same time, the residents may find their health improved by the greater wholesomeness of their food; and, before that, their minds will have become stirred and enlarged by intercourse with strangers who have, from circumstances, more vivacity of faculty and a wider knowledge. The best as well as the last and greatest change in the Lake District is that which is arising from the introduction of the railroad."

In the same year that her 'Guide to the Lakes' was published (1855), she completed her autobiography, although she was only in her early 50s and lived a further 21 years. Nearly all of her writing by now was of a non-fictional nature, and one important work was a detailed piece of research into the origins of religions, which she called 'Eastern Life'.

She was always abreast of contemporary affairs and was at heart a historian. Her 'History of the Thirty Years of Peace' analysed the years 1816 – 1846, a work that embodied the views of the philosophic radicals. The sheer versatility of her writing was remarkable. 'Forest and Game Law Tales' preceded the 'Thirty Years of Peace', and was followed by 'Letters on the Laws of Man's Social Nature'.

In 1853 she condensed Comte's 'Positive Philosophy' so successfully that the learned man recommended her version to his followers rather than his own! She had an unusually clear and vigorous intellect, and it is as an expositor and populariser of the opinions of others that she earned for herself a worthy position in the literature of the 19th century.

To the people of Ambleside she was anything but a remote intellectual. She was a familiar figure in the town, talking with everyone and especially popular with children. They were often up at The Knoll, shouting into her ear trumpet for a piece of material for their kites, or playing hide-and-seek in her garden.

The garden at The Knoll was not much better than an overgrown jungle. In the middle of it was a sundial with the inscription, 'Come, Light, Visit Me', but it was a forlorn hope as it was surrounded by 40 trees. The sundial eventually had its wish, for these were cut down almost half a century after her death.

This occurred in 1876, when she was 74, and Ambleside mourned her with spontaneous sadness. The ordinary folk of the town greatly missed the old lady in the lace cap, whose lively brain and sound common sense overcame her physical disabilities with such astonishing bravery. May she rest in peace. She was, as Charlotte Bronte observed, a great and a good lady.

FRANCES ELIZABETH COX
"Who are these like stars appearing?"

Two of the most distinguished translators of German hymns into English in the 19th century were women. One was Frances Elizabeth Cox and the other Catherine Winkworth, fifteen years her junior and featured in Volume 2.

Frances was born in Oxford in 1812, the daughter of George Cox. The quality of her translations was brought to light when she was 29, for in that year she published her 'Sacred Hymns from the German' which contained 49 translations. She published a second edition 23 years later that consisted of 56 hymns, some of her previous ones being omitted.

"Who are these like stars appearing?" was originally written by the German 17th century poet, Heinrich Theobald Schenck and was based on the 7th chapter of the Book of Revelations. The first two verses pose the question who are the multitude standing before the throne of God, wearing robes of the purest white and crowned with golden crowns?

The final three verses answer the question. They are the glorious band who persevered through anguish and woe, refusing to give in to mortal temptations. Day and night they laboured in God's service. But now "God has bid them weep no more," and they stand in His presence. The tune that is associated with this fine hymn is 'All Saints', composed by Darmstadt Gesangbuch in 1698.

Another well known translation by Frances Cox is "Jesus lives! Thy terrors now," featured in Volume 3 under its German author, Christian Gellert. He was a college professor in the 18th century, the son of a Lutheran minister. He intended to follow his father into Holy Orders, but as a young man he was so nervous and shy that his preaching suffered from hesitancy and stammering. Instead he became Professor of Philosophy at Leipzig, where he was enormously popular among the students.

Gellert was renowned for his generosity. Later in his life when Germany wa gripped by famine and beggars thronged the streets in droves, he gave awa all he owned and became destitute himself. When Prince Henry of Prussi was in Leipzig he asked for an audience with this scholar and poet, abou whom he had heard so much. He found him in a cold attic with very littl furniture and no food. Gellert is buried at Leipzig, next to an even mor illustrious figure, J.S. Bach.

In her 'Sacred Hymns from the German', Frances Cox not only provide translations of a high quality but also biographical notes on the origina German poets. Other translations include "Sing praise to God who reign above" from the German of Johann Jakob Schutz (1640 – 1690) and "O le him whose sorrow," a funeral hymn by Heinrich Siegmund Oswald, one tim reader to King Friedrich Willhelm II of Prussia. Two others that were onc popular are "A new and contrite heart create," and "Heavenward still ou pathway tends" by R. Schmolke.

Frances Cox did write some hymns of her own, which were published in th Victorian religious periodicals such as 'The Fireside', but she neve published a collection of them. She died in 1897 at Headington, only couple of miles or so from where she was born. She was then an old lady o 85, and English hymnody was the richer for her scholarly researches int some of the treasures of German sacred verse.

ROBERT MURRAY McCHEYNE
"I once was a stranger to grace and to God"

Robert Murray McCheyne was a Scottish pastor who in the course of his life of a mere 29 years achieved a legendary status as a man of utter holiness. The memory of his ministry in Dundee is still revered over one-and-a-half centuries after his death.

He was born in Edinburgh in 1813, and showed himself to be a child of unusual talent. At the age of four, while recovering from an illness, he asked for a slate on which he wrote the entire Greek alphabet. A year later he was entertaining the family to incessant poetical recitations.

In 1821 at the age of eight he entered Edinburgh High School, where he distinguished himself in Geography and poetry. He enrolled in Edinburgh University at the age of fourteen, where he added the study of languages to his curriculum. Out of the classroom he indulged in sketching, music and gymnastics, for which he was particularly suited by his slight frame. He also enjoyed evenings on the town in company with his fellow undergraduates.

In 1831 his eldest brother David died, an event which affected him deeply. For the rest of his life he commemorated the anniversary of David's death by fasting and prayer. It was really the event which was the start of Robert's own spiritual awakening.

Aged eighteen at this time, he read 'The Sum of Saving Knowledge', a popular Scottish tract of the period, which convinced him to dedicate his life to bringing Christ into the life of others. This was reaffirmed when he read H. Martyn's 'Memoirs', which inspired him to write in his journal: "Would I could imitate him, giving up father, mother, country, home, health, life, all – for Christ! And yet, what hinders? Lord, purify me, and give me strength to dedicate myself, my all, to Thee!"

In 1831, still aged only eighteen, he entered the Divinity Hall of Edinburgh University to prepare for his sacred calling. Some of his society friends of a more frivolous nature were surprised, and from a few of them he had to face derision.

He joined some of his fellow students in visiting some of the darkest tenements of Edinburgh to communicate the good news of the Gospel. These dark courts and alleys were seldom visited by a minister or outsiders.

Robert was studying Jewish literature at this time, and it was while he was laid up with fever in 1834 that he wrote his hymn 'Jehovah Tsidkenu'. It is featured in detail later in this chapter.

The following year, when he was 21, he was licensed by the Presbytery of Annan to preach the Gospel. He preached his first sermon at Ruthwell Church, near Dumfries, and took for his subject the Pool of Bethesda. For the first ten months of his ministry he acted as assistant to the Rev'd. John Bonar, the minister of Larbert and Dunipace, near Stirling. It was a time of much earnest prayer and serious reading.

In November 1836 Robert was appointed minister of St. Peter's, Dundee. The parishioners were in a very low spiritual condition, and although the congregation numbered 1,100 from a parish of 4,000 people, about 400 of these came from outside the parish. He tried to take heed of ALL his flock by instituting evening classes for the young, many of whom could not read.

They studied their Bibles and learnt their Catechisms under the guidance of their young minister, and he also started weekly prayer meetings in church. Soon he started to receive many enquirers from those who were not members of his congregation, and these folk he instructed in his own house.

ROBERT MURRAY McCHEYNE

Robert was particular about only administering the sacraments and baptisin; members of families who were earnest and sincere about their beliefs Within a few months, vast numbers from all over Dundee and beyon flocked to St. Peter's. He preached in a clear voice with an attractive style o delivery, and although he was so youthful he had a compelling presence i the pulpit. His constant theme was Christ, the personal, living Saviour, eve present with the faithful and ever waiting to receive sinners.

Around the town Robert McCheyne was always careful to deport himself a was becoming for a minister. Every word and every act was carefull measured. Constantly he received offers from country parishes with smalle populations and higher stipends to offer, but he decided that as God wa blessing his work in Dundee, he would remain there.

Throughout his ministry McCheyne was a regular attender at meetings c presbytery. He spoke with great wisdom during the troubled times of th disruption of the Scottish Church in 1843 and the formation of the Fre Church in Scotland. He believed ardently that the Church should be entirel independent of the civil power in spiritual matters.

McCheyne's health had never been robust, and in 1838 it broke dow completely. He was forced to take a complete rest from his parochial dutie: This allowed him to spend time in study and contemplation, although he ha the urge to be "up and doing yet more abundantly, seeing that the time i short."

Nevertheless, he made good use of his enforced break. He wrote in h journal: "I always feel it is a blessed thing when the Saviour takes me asid from the crowd, and removes the veil, and clears away obscuring mists, an by his word and spirit leads to deeper peace and a holier walk."

At the time of his recuperation a committee of the Church of Scotlan decided to send a deputation of four to Palestine to see what might be done i setting up missionary operations among the Jews. McCheyne was invited join the deputation. He accepted with alacrity, for he had long cherished desire to be active in foreign missionary work.

They went first to Paris, where McCheyne was appalled at the profanation of the Sabbath which was rife there. Then they journeyed via Alexandria to Palestine by way of the desert. He was deeply impressed by the loneliness of the wilderness which they crossed by camel, and for the first time he realised the hardships that had caused the Israelites to murmur against Moses in ancient times.

"If Christians more frequently found themselves in circumstances somewhat similar to those in which, perhaps they are accustomed to condemn the conduct of God's ancient people," he wrote, "it is quite a question whether they would not be as likely to murmur as were the Israelites."

When the party neared Jerusalem, McCheyne urged his camel to advance ahead of the others so that he could have first sight of the city. From there they proceeded to Hebron, Samaria and Carmel, and then to Galilee. They moved on to Constantinople and returned to Scotland through Austrian Poland and Prussia. A report was submitted to the General Assembly in 1840, as a result of which it was resolved that the cause of Israel should form one of the great missionary schemes of the Church of Scotland.

St. Peter's had been very well served during McCheyne's absence by the Rev'd. W.C. Burns, the minister who had been left in charge. He had instituted a religious revival at Kilsyth, which had spread to Dundee with remarkable results.

So well were matters progressing in his own parish that McCheyne felt able to go on preaching tours with a small group of fellow ministers. They went first to Ireland and later to Newcastle, which one of them described at the time as "a town giving itself up to utter godlessness."

In 1843 McCheyne went by himself on another preaching tour, often speaking in the open air after hours on horseback in freezing temperatures. At Lintrathen the people offered to stop work at mid-day if he would come and preach to them. In February of that year he went off to Deer and Ellon, north of Aberdeen, where in three weeks he spoke at meetings in 24 places. The deep solemnity of his preaching deeply touched his congregations, who felt they were in the presence of a very holy man.

Dr. Bonar wrote that there were two aspects of McCheyne's life that he held paramount: his most anxious efforts to save souls, and his cultivation of personal holiness. With regard to the latter, McCheyne prepared a document for his own perusal, in which he stressed how important it was to spend the best hours of the day in communion with God. In private prayer he felt it essential to include all of the key contents of confession, adoration, thanksgiving, petition and intercession.

In the pulpit or in the town square, wherever he chose to speak, he presented a most commanding figure. He was tall and slight, with penetrating but kindly eyes and a most melodious voice. In character he showed a happy combination of firmness and gentleness, and a maturity of wisdom well beyond his years. This he acquired through rigorous self-discipline, countless hours of study and a large part of his day devoted to prayer.

McCheyne always prepared himself for the pulpit with deep contemplation. His sermons often contained ardent personal appeals to his congregation. He ended one of them with the words:

"I would here then take occasion to make offer of Christ with all his benefits to every soul in this assembly. To every man and woman and child I do now, in the name of my Master, make full, free offer of a crucified Saviour to be your surety and righteousness, your refuge and strength. I would let down the Gospel cord so low, that sinners who are low of stature, like Zaccheus, may lay hold of it. Oh, is there none will lay hold of Christ, the only Saviour?"

His sermons were sometimes too long, and he could be rather impatient. His aim was to procure immediate results, which often was not the most productive policy. But no lesser judge than Dr. Bonar wrote of him: "During the six short years of his ministry, he was the instrument of saving more souls than many true servants of God have done during half a century."

Robert McCheyne's hymns were published in his 'Songs of Zion' in Dundee in 1843. All were composed between the years 1831 – 1841, and some were written in Palestine. The best known, which was particularly popular in America, is "I once was a stranger to grace and to God," which was entitled 'Jehovah Tsidkenu', meaning 'The Lord our righteousness'. It first appeared in the 'Scottish Christian Herald' in 1836. It shows its author as a poet of much ability as well as a very holy man, and as it is virtually out of print now, it is worth setting out in its entirety:

"I once was a stranger to grace and to God.
I knew not my danger and felt not my load;
Though friends spoke in rapture of Christ on the tree,
Jehovah Tsidkenu was nothing to me.
I oft read with pleasure, to soothe or engage,
Isaiah's wild measure and John's simple page;
But e'en when they pictured the blood-sprinkled tree,
Jehovah Tsidkenu seemed nothing to me.

Like tears from the daughters of Zion that roll,
I wept when the waters went over his soul;
Yet thought not that my sins had nailed to the tree
Jehovah Tsidkenu – 'twas nothing to me.

When free grace awoke me by light from on high,
Then legal fears shook me, I trembled to die;
No refuge, no safety in self could I see,
Jehovah Tsidkenu my Saviour must be.

My terrors all vanished before the sweet name;
My guilty fears banished, with boldness I came
To drink of the fountain, life-giving and free,
Jehovah Tsidkenu is all things to me.

Jehovah Tsidkenu! My treasure and boast,
Jehovah Tsidkenu! I ne'er can be lost;
In Thee I shall conquer by flood and by field!
My cable, my anchor, my breast-plate and shield!

Even treading the valley, the shadow of death,
This watchword shall rally my faltering breath;
For while from life's fever my God sets me free,
Jehovah Tsidkenu my death-song shall be."

The hymn was included in 'Sacred Songs and Solos', the hymnal compiled by Moody and Sankey for their mission meetings.

McCheyne returned from his winter preaching tour early in 1843 absolutely exhausted, but he still insisted upon preaching three times on the following Sunday. His parish was rife with typhoid, and he spent most of his time visiting the inflicted. The following week he was struck down with fever himself, and he never recovered. He died in March 1843, aged only 29.

The effect of his death on the town of Dundee was remarkable. Crowds gathered at the church, and the wailing of the people could be heard a long way off. On the day of McCheyne's funeral, not a single business in the town opened, and so many people attended that a simultaneous service had to be held outside as well as inside the church.

In the funeral oration the Rev'd. J. Roxburgh said of him: "Whether viewed as a son, a brother, a friend or a pastor, often has the remark been made by those who knew him most intimately, that he was the most faultless and attractive exhibition of the true Christian which they had ever seen embodied in a human form."

He was buried in his own churchyard of St. Peter's, and the monument erected over his grave gives fitting reference to his remarkable ministry. It states: "Walking closely with God, an example of the believers in word, in conversation, in charity, in spirit, in faith, in purity, he ceased not day and night to labour and watch for souls, and was honoured by his Lord to draw many wanderers out of darkness into the path of life."

WILLIAM PENNEFATHER
"Jesus, stand among us in thy risen power"

William Pennefather was not a great hymn-writer but he was a remarkable parish priest and an inspirational Christian, whose life is an interesting record of the very best type of Victorian clergyman.

He was born in Merrion Square, Dublin, in 1816. His father was an eminent Irish judge and his mother, Jane, the daughter of an equally distinguished judge. He was devoted to her, and for a while in his early ministry in Ireland, she came to live with him. William was the youngest of eight children, but although suffering from ill-health throughout his life, he outlived them all.

He was educated at a prep. school near Dublin until he was thirteen and then at Westbury College, near Bristol, where he was spoken of in later years as 'the saintly boy'. He made a remarkable impression at Westbury, so much so that Mrs. Fry, the headmaster's wife, had a picture of him at the foot of her bed until her dying day.

Even at school his thoughts dwelt more on religious matters than they did on football and cricket. He held a Bible class in one of the smaller dormitories, and earned the love and admiration of many of his colleagues. William showed great sensitivity even to the meanest of God's creatures, and could not bear even to tread on a worm.

It was inevitable that he should be teased for his pious nature at a boys' boarding school. But four of the bullies sought him out well after schooldays were over, to ask his pardon. One beseeched him on his knees, and all claimed to have acquired their faith through his example.

William left school when he was sixteen and was placed under the charge of the Rev'd. William Stephens at Levens, near Kendal. His report back to the judge in Dublin read: "When he stirs up his mind he exhibits more than ordinary acuteness, uniting with the simplicity and playfulness of a child the thoughtfulness of age."

It was while he was there that he first met a couple who were to become close life-long friends, Mr. and Mrs. Crewdson of Sizergh Hall, near Levens. He was able to share with them their love of painting, music and in particular poetry, for they were all living amidst the haunts of Wordsworth, Southey and Coleridge.

He entered Trinity College, Dublin, when he was eighteen but was immediately struck down by ill health. He had to return to the family house in Dublin as it was feared he was suffering from consumption, and there he was lovingly nursed by his sister Susan while the rest of the family went off to their usual summer haunt in Co. Tipperary. When he was 21 Pennefather did return to Trinity College, although he had to live at home because of his health. He graduated B.A. three years later.

Despite the fact that he was the most loving of souls, who had a quite unique communion with God for a young man, already we see instances of his antagonism towards Roman Catholics. It was a normal Protestant trait in those days when the Church of England was so shaken by the precepts of the Oxford Movement, but nevertheless it comes as a shock to find him of all people referring to some converts in Co. Kerry in the following terms: "There have been a few who have hazarded their lives for the truth's sake, have left Popery and joined themselves to the true Church, like a gleam of sunshine in the midst of a storm."

Pennefather was ordained in 1841 at Durham by Dr. Sumner, Bishop of Chester and later to become Archbishop of Canterbury. He preached his first sermon at Levens, in front of his Westmorland friends. Meanwhile the rector of Balymacugh had offered him a curacy, without a stipend but with a house provided. He thought Co. Cavan rather too comfortable a place, having in mind real missionary work off the west coast on Arran Island.

He accepted the curacy and in September 1841 started his ministry at Balymacugh. He set about his work with characteristic diligence, needing considerable powers of perseverance for the parishioners were not the sort to indulge in dramatic conversions. He wrote of his flock: "They are grossly ignorant and careless, many of them sunk in poverty and wretchedness, but I have found some bright jewels among the multitude."

Considering the frail nature of his health, he lived a remarkably hectic life. He took an active interest in missionary work in Connemara and was frequently journeying to those parts. He also made a trip to Paris to visit a sick sister, and journeys to Dublin on missionary work were frequent.

Christmas 1843 found him very busy in the parish, trying to clothe the poor for the winter, which was very severe. There was great poverty in the parish, and in a letter he wrote "The country is in a fearful state." But despite his wonderful work among the poor at Balymacugh, he felt that it was time for his ministry there to come to an end. He was offered the living at Mellifont, three miles from Drogheda, which had a stipend of £92 per annum, ten acres of land and "a very neat house."

One of his parishioners at Balymacugh gave an insight into his work there in this tribute: "Besides constantly visiting his people, he was at all times at their call. His intense anxiety for those who were at any sickness or sorrow was well known, and his deep loving sympathy was constantly sought, and never sought in vain. His health needed much care, but it was the last thing he thought of, and often on my going to the cottage, the servants would come to me with the complaint, 'O, sir, Mr. Pennefather is killing himself.'"

Mellifont was a big parish with a population of 4,500, but few of them were Protestants, and they were scattered over a wide area. This made pastoral work particularly tiring. But it was close to the new Drogheda rail link with Dublin, which was a real bonus. Pennefather regarded his ministry there as a time of trial and discouragement, and he was often lonely. He missed his mother who had died recently while living with him at Balymacugh, and his sister Susan who had died in childbirth.

He started an afternoon service there as well as a morning one, but his flock was so dispersed that the congregation was inevitably small. Even his own parsonage failed to give him any pleasure. "My predecessors did not care for anything pretty," he wrote, "and the garden is full of potatoes. The place is truly Irish in its confusion, dirt and negligence. I feel as if everything were so wholly gone to ruin that it is hopeless to think of repairing it. I trust I shall not be shackled by the cares of an evil world!"

By getting to know his flock in the intimate surroundings of their homes he found that numbers increased in the more formal church services. But in 1846 increased weakness forced him to see a doctor, who demanded immediate cessation from his parochial work. He went to England for a period of recuperation, and then on to Langen-Schwalbach in Germany.

When he returned to Ireland in the autumn of 1846 he found the whole country groaning under the scourge of famine, due to the repeated failure of the potato crops. Starvation was rife in the west and south, and even in the east around Mellifont, the peasantry were largely at the mercy of the resident gentry and Catholic clergy, who were the land-owners.

Writing in November of that year he remarked: "The money sent has been a most timely assistance, for even here the poverty is great. It is wages the people want; food there is at present, if there were money to purchase it. On Monday I was at the relief committee, and pinching hunger was too plainly written on the faces of many of the people. I am going to drain a field I have, to make walks, etc., to try and find employment for a few…"

Pennefather's next venture was to open a mission school at Clough Patrick, in his parish. Well aware that Protestant numbers had made virtually no impact on the Catholic population, he purchased the largest cottage in the village and fitted it up, providing a residence for the school-mistress beside it. By 1847 numbers had risen to 80, and children's voices could be heard singing hymns of praise along the road instead of the previous constant sound of angry curses.

In the summer of 1847 he had a most important commitment at Cranbrook in Kent. He had met Catherine, eldest daughter of Admiral King, when she had been staying with her brother William, the rector of Delgany and a friend of William Pennefather's. The wedding took place at Cranbrook and the honeymoon in the Lake District was a brief respite before the realism of another winter in a land in crisis.

By November the couple were back at Mellifont, where famine fever was rampant. The Protestant population suffered less than the other villagers as they were looked after by their minister and the few more wealthy members of the congregation. But it was a sad sight to witness the indolent endurance

Waiting for meal at Mellifont Glebe

with which hundreds of ragged creatures would sit from morn till night, around any dwelling where they had the faintest hope of obtaining a slice of bread.

As winter came on, Mellifont Glebe was besieged by crowds once the word got around that meal was served out daily. Many of the gentry looked upon this as folly, as its overall effect was negligible amidst the ocean of misery all around. But William and Catherine were unable to shut their doors and their hearts in the face of this catastrophe, and no doubt there were other good souls who acted in the same way.

Although Pennefather found his work at Mellifont discouraging at times, his efforts had not gone unobserved by the Church of England in a place far removed from Ireland. In 1848 he received a letter from the trustees of Trinity Church, Walton, a parish in Aylesbury, inviting him to be their new incumbent. He had intended to devote his life's work to Ireland, but he now felt that the Lord required his services in England. He wrote to his father in Dublin whom he thought would strongly oppose a move from Ireland, but the old man simply replied that he should do as the Lord willed.

The Aylesbury parish was described as being a difficult place with no worldly attractions, a very small income and no society. But the trustees stressed that there was infinite scope for labour, and perhaps it was this that induced Pennefather to take up the challenge. He did not even waste time in going to see the place.

He found Walton to be a suburb of Aylesbury, with about 900 parishioners. The church was only three years old and could lay claim to no architectural beauty. Aylesbury itself was far from being a pretty place, and was situated in a wide, tree-less plain. In March the landscape around the town was one of interminable ploughed fields.

The congregation, who came from all over the town, was friendly but reserved. Initially they were wary of a new incumbent from Ireland. Two special needs immediately confronted him. There was no education for the children of the poor, and most of his congregation was certainly in this category. The majority of them were agricultural workers, and many of the women reared ducks for the London market. Straw-plaiting and lace making were other cottage industries.

The second need was for a ministry among the bargemen operating on the Grand Union Canal, who had their hovels around the wharf. The men were begrimed with coal dust, and their families led an itinerant existence either travelling with the barges or at home around the wharf.

At once Pennefather set to work collecting subscriptions for a church school, spurred on by the knowledge that the Roman Catholics had purchased land near Trinity Church for their own church and schools. These in fact were never built. But in a letter to a friend, he wrote: "While men sleep the enemy is sowing tares. Pray that the Lord may bless our efforts to train up the children in His faith and fear." It is strange that a man of such love and sensitivity should continue to show such vindictiveness towards those who worshipped the same God.

For the conversion of the bargemen he persuaded a dear friend who was an ardent evangelist to come and live among the men and their families for some weeks. By means of outdoor preaching and close personal contact, this good soul did a fine missionary job among the itinerant community.

Meanwhile, Pennefather's own parochial efforts were reaping great reward. The church, built to accommodate 450, was soon crammed with 550 – 600 for the Sunday evening service, and a room in an empty house was used for prayer-meetings during the week. This was invariably crammed with new worshippers.

As the winter of 1849 advanced an outbreak of cholera alarmed the area, but strangely not a single death occurred in Aylesbury. The new school was completed and duly opened, and church attendances continued to swell. At last he and Catherine were able to move out of their lodgings into their own house.

He described it in a letter to Mrs. Crewdson: "We are settling into our funny little house. Though it is dignified with the name of Walton House, it has only one bedroom, and attics in the roof. It stands in a garden and, strange to say, has gates and a lodge, which we are fitting up for classes." He was also at that time appointed chaplain to the Union Workhouse, a position that he welcomed. It also brought him in an extra £40 per annum, which allowed him to employ a curate. Without one he had to preach three sermons every Sunday.

By 1850 Pennefather had established day schools with 150 in attendance, a Sunday school with 150 and a night school for men and women which attracted 110. There was a prayer meeting on Friday evenings generally attended by about 80. In addition there were Sunday classes for men and women, and a Young Men's Association. No wonder he needed a curate!

All this did not go unobserved. The following year he was approached by Captain Trotter, a man who was to become a close personal friend for the rest of his life. The Captain invited Pennefather to take up a post in Barnet. He left Aylesbury with deep sorrow in his heart, but with the inner conviction that it was time to move on.

Pennefather wrote to his flock: "Your unwearied kindness has often gladdened our hearts, and nothing but the clearest indication that God is removing us could bear us up under the trial now before us." The deep silent grief of the people, as the time of separation drew near, was even more touching than the loud demonstrations of sorrow and the stifled sobs that made the services almost oppressive.

After some delay Pennefather commenced his ministry at Christ Church, Barnet, in December 1852. His new parsonage was only ten miles from London, which was convenient for attending committee meetings. The new house had no garden, only a bare plot of land, which was a matter of some regret to William, and no doubt to Catherine as well.

The closeness to London gave the town a character of restlessness and hurry, with many of his congregation constantly scampering off to London for their employment. This afforded little time for personal fellowship, which was so beloved by Pennefather. But the congregation was united by a strong bond of Christian fellowship, and increased rapidly.

In 1856 the first Barnet Conference was held, in which ministers and missionaries from different sects were invited to pray together and attend lectures and discussion groups over four days. It was a bold venture, but representatives of twelve different denominations of the Christian Church attended. They even came together for a Holy Communion service on the final day, conducted from the Church of England prayer book.

The inter-denominational Conference was held annually throughout his time at Barnet and in his next parish as well. It was held in the church, the parsonage, the school house and the meeting room, overflowing on fine days even into the parsonage garden. This soon became no longer a bare plot but a verdant oasis of colour. It must have given Catherine a major domestic burden, but she took it all in her stride.

By 1858 delegates arrived from the Church of England, the Baptists, Independents, Wesleyans, Moravians, Plymouth Brethren, Church of Scotland (Established and Free), Dutch Reformed Church, Lutherans and the Society of Friends. William presided over the whole affair, and one Quaker described him in these words:

"His whole attitude and bearing, with the benignity of his countenance, seemed a personification of Christian love... His deep humility was very marked, for he had learnt of Him who was meek and lowly of heart, and as he took his place in the centre of the Conference platform, or moved about in friendly intercourse, it was evident that he came fresh from hallowed communion with his Lord... There was an irresistible attractiveness and purity about him that drew us towards him with reverent love..."

Pennefather spent so much of his time visiting his parishioners in need that it is remarkable he ever found time to cope with a daunting correspondence. There were always sermons to plan, letters about committee matters, notes of comfort to the sick and advice to be given to friends who sought it by post. Then, after a harrowing day about the streets of Barnet, he would quite often go to his desk and write a hymn for the orphanage or maybe his Sunday school to sing the following Sunday.

He and Catherine often had guests staying at the parsonage. These came from a number of European countries as well as India, China and Africa. But he did have the assistance of the Rev'd. F.A. Baines, his curate, for most of his time at Barnet. The two men had a close working relationship, and enjoyed each other's company.

There was now desperate need for a large room that would serve the needs of the summer Conference and be used for prayer meetings with the poor in the winter months. In recent years those who had come to the Conference without invitations had to be turned away. Pennefather determined to go to London to see what could be done, and in the train met his old friend Captain Trotter. When he heard of William's mission, the Captain immediately wrote a cheque for £100 to commence the undertaking.

The building measured 100 ft. by 60 ft. and was largely prefabricated. It was constructed in the middle of a field, which necessitated access roads to be built. Building started in November, and as the money flooded in it was opened before Christmas. 1,100 people assembled there for the inauguration, most of them from the poorer section of the parish.

Special services were held in the iron room (as the new building was called) which had an extraordinary effect on the town. People of every class flocked to the building. Men and women appeared who had never been seen in a church before, and the pubs were relatively empty. Hundreds were moved to tears by the simple message of the gospel, and after the services they remained for prayer and conversation. There were no histrionics or dramatic conversions, simply earnest prayer and fellowship. The meetings went on for ten weeks, with Pennefather nearly always presiding.

Despite his prolific programme of commitments in the parish, he still found time in most years to go on a preaching circuit. In 1862 he visited Sheffield and Liverpool before going on to the cotton towns of Lancashire which were suffering from the so-called 'cotton famine'. He preached in the Corn Exchange, Manchester and the parish church in Blackburn, now the city's cathedral, which was full with 1,200 people. He liked Blackburn, despite its dismal exterior, and found its people hungering and thirsting after righteousness.

But it was not to Blackburn that he went to work next but to London. Both he and Catherine felt that their work was done in Barnet, and now they had an earnest supplication from St. Jude's, Mildmay Park, in North London. To

William's delight this was in a depressed part of the city, and his parishioners were nearly all poor people.

In April 1864 he delivered his final sermons at St. Jude's. There was no parsonage at Mildmay Park but the people were kind and responsive, welcoming them with love in their hearts. Congregations, however, were small, and not many of the churchgoers were from the poorer homes. One of his first tasks was to remove the huge iron room from Barnet and erect it on a piece of waste ground in the parish. Considering there were no cranes, lorries or even adequate roads, it was an amazing undertaking.

Pennefather started an orphanage for 40 boys at Hackney, which soon grew to 80. He built schools for the children of the poor, and opened daily soup kitchens. Both were now well settled, and William had the help of two curates. Early in 1865 he wrote to a friend, "My mouth is filled with praise for the mercies which our Heavenly Father has showered down upon us here. We are very happy in our work. It is a delightful sphere of labour."

Later that year they paid their first visit to Switzerland with a disabled sister of Catherine's who needed to recuperate. William at once fell in love with the Alps, and arose at 4 a.m. to watch the first rays of the sun strike the snowy peak of Mont Blanc.

Back at Mildmay it was a familiar story. The church was packed, and money-raising initiatives allowed buildings to be bought for new schools and missions. As each busy year went past the number of earnest worshippers continued to increase, and many who had previously been indifferent or even hostile now came to be involved.

One of his parishioners wrote about his experience of being with Pennefather at this time: "When walking with him in the poor parts of the parish it was a very pretty thing to see the bright look of joy that spread over the faces of young and old as they caught his smile of recognition, and to hear the welcomes that greeted him as he looked in at the cottage doors."

Most of his hymns were written for the 1866 and 1867 Conferences. These he produced in a volume entitled 'Original Hymns and Thoughts in Verse'. One of the most popular was No. 22 in this book, "O Saviour we adore

Thee," but the one that has survived to be included in some of the modern hymnals is:

> "Jesus, stand among us
> In thy risen pow'r;
> Let this time of worship
> Be a hallowed hour."

It is normally set to the tune 'Caswall', composed by Friedrich Filitz, a contemporary of Pennefather's. It can also be sung to 'Linton' by Walter Stanton.

By 1868 the need for a bigger mission hall had become very apparent. This would act as a headquarters for the annual Conference, and as a venue for afternoon and evening services on Sundays for the non-church-going population. It would also be used for children's services, for the church was now quite inadequate to accommodate the numbers who came flocking to the doors. Pennefather also envisaged it as a meeting place for home and overseas evangelists who came to London in the course of their work. He planned it to incorporate a large room for social meetings.

Every Sunday he now had eight services to plan, with the help of his curates. But he still made time for his preaching tours, and with energy that defied his indifferent health he set off that summer to visit his old friend Mrs. Crewdson. From there he went to Keswick, always a hot-bed of evangelism, and then on to Scotland, where he preached in Perth and the Free Assembly Hall in Edinburgh.

On his return he spotted a plot of nursery ground that would be ideal for his proposed mission hall. When passing the spot a week or two later he noticed a sign stating that this and some neighbouring land was up for sale, due to the death of a member of the Mildmay family who owned it.

A lady had recently handed Pennefather a cheque for £500, remarking that she was much distressed by the present crowded state of the church. He therefore instructed his man of business to go to the auction and bid up to £500 for the land, "but not a penny more." The bidding opened at £100 and moved relentlessly on to £490. Then there was a pause, and William's man of business nodded nonchalantly at the auctioneer. No further bids were forthcoming, so the land was marked down to Pennefather for the exact sum of £500. As he said afterwards, "I felt it was the Lord's doing, and it was marvellous in our eyes!"

On his birthday, 5th February 1869, he was sitting in his study opening his post when he came across a letter enclosing a cheque for £1,000 from one of his parishioners. This was afterwards increased to £5,000 and was for the mission hall building fund. Work began on what was now called the Mildmay Conference Hall, which Pennefather intended to be a centre of light and mission effort for the whole of North London. The building was to contain a large hall to seat 2,5oo for meetings and Conferences, and underneath it there were to be classrooms and a kitchen.

In the summer of 1870 friends begged him to take a holiday on the Continent, as it was impossible to cease entirely from work anywhere in England. He and Catherine spent some time at Zurich, from where he wrote regularly to his congregation. "I am thinking often of the poor of London," he wrote, "and the sick ones in their hot rooms." He returned in time for the opening of the Conference Hall, and the 1870 Conference which was its first main event.

Although he now had a team of curates and parish helpers to assist with parochial care, visits to the sick and dying were largely undertaken by Pennyfather himself. In the final years of his life his doctor remarked, "He ought not to be much in sick-rooms, but I don't know how to forbid it: it is a work for which he is so eminently calculated. He once visited me in an illness, and I shall never forget it."

Every now and then the Pennyfathers were able to snatch a few hours of peace by retiring to a little house at Richmond which they had owned for some little while. They now decided to sell it and buy another at Muswell Hill, where the air was more bracing. It was close enough to the parish for members of the congregation to spend the day there, in groups of a dozen or so. They talked, strolled about the garden and prayed together, a living example of Christian fellowship that was so precious to all who experienced it. One poor woman on her death-bed confided to a lady who visited her, "The very happiest earthly day I ever spent was when twelve of us communicants from St. Jude's went off to Mr. Pennefather's house."

WILLIAM PENNEFATHER

In the spring of 1871 it was finally decided that the chancel of St. Jude's should be enlarged, to relieve the overcrowding at Sunday services. While the work was taking place services were held in the Conference Hall. Funds came pouring in for the work. William and Catherine returned from Switzerland in time to plan the re-opening of the church when the enlargement was complete.

It could now accommodate an additional 400 people, and the consecration service took place in December 1871. Despite the rows of new pews the enlarged church was as crowded as ever, with chairs and benches filling up the vacant spaces. There were also 1,392 children enrolled in the church day schools and 1,249 in the Sunday school.

William's declining health was only too obvious as 1872 advanced. He and Catherine spent most nights at the house in Muswell Hill, coming up by day to work in the parish. Several of those who attended Conference that year foresaw that he stood there on the platform for the last time.

In the late summer Catherine and William paid another visit to Germany and Switzerland, as it turned out a last chance to gaze at their beloved Alps. William struggled on with the usual winter routine of night schools, tea meetings, Christmas gatherings and so forth, but it was obvious his health and strength were slipping from him. In mid-February his Sunday sermon at St. Jude's was a struggle, and many there foretold that it would be the last time he would preach. So it proved to be, for his doctor insisted that he and Catherine should go and live at their cottage at Muswell Hill.

William found as the year progressed that he was suffering from mental fatigue as well as physical, and to his great distress for the first time in his life he found this even in prayer. He managed one more visit to his parsonage at Mildmay, but he was unable to meet his friends. Early in May he died at Muswell Hill aged 57, and was buried at Ridge, near Barnet, next to his dearest friend Captain Trotter.

Tributes to him appeared in many of the Christian publications, a particularly apt one being published in 'Church Bells'. After detailing his many practical achievements, the writer pays tribute to his personal character in these words:

"He was pre-eminently a man of love. Such was his natural amiability that none could know him without loving him; but to this he added the aggressive power of true Christian charity. Completely devoted to his Master's service, blessed with a wonderfully childlike faith, and possessing a habit of constant prayer, the man's whole life was a perpetual sermon, which spoke to the heart much more forcibly than any words. How highly he was valued was proved by the affecting sorrow of the multitude who thronged around his remains. The sight of that vast sobbing congregation as their beloved pastor's remains were borne up the aisle for the last time is one that will never be erased from the memory."

GEORGE HUNT SMYTTAN
"Forty days and forty nights"

As a young child I always found "Forty days and forty nights" rather frightening. To start with the tune is decidedly doleful, as indeed it should be for a penitential hymn. Also some of the imagery does not leave a lot to the imagination.

The vision of scorching sunbeams, chilly dew-drops, prowling beasts and stone pillows was quite harrowing enough for one day, let alone forty days and forty nights. And the final nightmare to chill a young mind wakeful in the dark night is contained in the couplet:

> "What if Satan, vexing sore,
> Flesh and spirit shall assail?"

In fact it is a very good hymn, with a stern reminder in verse 3 of the self-discipline that Christians should practise during the season of Lent:

> "Shall not we thy sorrow share,
> Learn thy discipline of will,
> And, like thee, by fast and prayer
> Wrestle with the powers of ill?"

It was first published in 'Penny Post' in 1856, under the heading 'Poetry for Lent'. The tune 'Heinlein', by Michael Heinlein, although it is also accredited to the 17th century composer Martin Herbert, is very suitable for a Lenten penitential hymn. It is solemn, slow and moves steadily down the scale as it progresses, a kind of musical illustration of "chilly dew-drops nightly shed." An alternative tune, 'Temptation', was composed by the 19th century clergyman, Canon F.A.J. Hervey.

The author of this hymn was George Hunt Smyttan, who was born in 1822. His father, Dr. Smyttan, was attached to the Bombay Medical Board, so it may have been that young George had a rather lonely childhood while his parents were in India. He went up to Corpus Christi College, Cambridge, and graduated in 1845.

In 1848 he was ordained and two years later was presented to the living of Hawksworth, an attractive village in the Vale of Belvoir in Nottinghamshire. Although not far from the M1 today, it is still in a bit of a backwater, in country lanes not many miles east of Nottingham.

The old rectory, which presumably was George Smyttan's abode, is now a low, rambling manor house, covered in creeper which is much favoured by nesting birds. It has a lovely garden, a mass of daffodils in spring and shaded by huge chestnut trees in summer. It is the perfect setting for rectory tea parties on the lawn, with perhaps the clink of croquet balls and the high-pitched laughter of young voices as yet another ball is dispatched with glee to some distant herbaceous border.

The house is by the church, which has a brick tower containing a treasure. Built into the wall of the tower is a Norman tympanum, encircled by roses and stars. In the middle is a cross, with two smaller crosses on either side bearing the effigies of the two thieves. There is also a Latin inscription, stating that the church was built by Walter and Cecilina his wife in the 12th century.

George Smyttan spent all his ministry in this happy place, remaining rector there for twenty years. He was only 48 when he died in 1870. He wrote one other hymn, "Jesu, ever present with thy Church below," and a volume entitled 'Thoughts in verse for the afflicted'. In a lighter vein were his 'Mission Songs and Ballads', for his was the county of Robin Hood, and ballads of the men of Sherwood Forest were an essential part of every local child's education.

WILLIAM BRIGHT
"And now, O Father, mindful of thy love"

Many Christians attending Communion services over the past 150 years will have been struck by the moving words of William Bright's hymn, "And now, O Father, mindful of thy love". It is really a hymn of preparation for receiving the Holy Sacraments, and it has about it an aura of holiness which makes it particularly suitable for that sacred occasion.

It reminds us of the anguish of Calvary, the Sacrifice prepared for us at the Last Supper and our own unworthiness to participate in the feast. It recalls our loved ones also in need of divine protection, and ends by reminding us of the momentous, sacred gift of the Holy Sacraments in the final verse:

> "And so we come, O draw us to thy feet,
>   Most patient Saviour, who canst love us still;
> And by this food, so awful and so sweet,
>   Deliver us from every touch of ill:
> In thine own service make us glad and free,
> And grant us never more to part with thee."

It can be sung either to 'Song 1' or 'Song 4' by Orlando Gibbons, a leading composer of church music in the late Tudor and early Stuart times who was also organist at Westminster Abbey at one time. An alternative tune is 'Unde et Memores' by William Henry Monk, the musical editor of the original edition of 'Hymns Ancient and Modern' and composer of 'Abide with Me'.

"And so we come," and a collection of other hymns as well, was written by William Bright, who was one of the leading ecclesiastical history academics of the Victorian era. He was born in Doncaster in 1824 and educated at University College, Oxford. He graduated in 1846 but while working on his MA he became the Johnson's Theological Scholar in 1847 and won the Ellerton Theological Essay prize in the following year.

He was elected a Fellow and later became Tutor of his college, and to no-one's surprise whatsoever he was ordained in 1848. For a decade or so he was Tutor at Glenalmond, one of the leading public schools in Scotland, but the calls of Oxford were never far from his heart, and he returned there in 1859. He became Regius Professor of Ecclesiastical History and Canon at Christ Church.

The excitement of the exertions of the Oxford Movement were still recent history at Oxford, and some of the dons most instrumental in the Movement in the 1830s would still have been in residence. But William Bright was, perhaps, more fascinated by the past than the present, and one pictures him occupying a large, panelled room with dusty and very weighty books filling every corner.

On the table by the door would, perhaps, be a pile of students' essays on the implications of the Synod of Whitby, waiting forlornly for his perusal, while on his desk might be notes and texts for one of his works on ancient church history. He was always working on some learned tome, involving painstaking research and a love of scholarship.

His works include a volume on ancient collects, and a colossal undertaking entitled 'History of the Church from the Edict of Milan to the Council of Chalcedon 1869'. Another historical work dealt with early English church history, and he published two volumes of devotional prayers, one for personal use and the other for family prayers.

William Bright died in 1901, at the age of 77. Two other hymns of his are sometimes found in modern hymnals, "At thy feet, O Christ, we lay" and "Once, only once, and once for all." Certainly his hymns deserve to live on, although probably his ecclesiastical historical works are never read today, even by the most conscientious theological student.

WALTER CHALMERS SMITH
"Immortal, invisible, God only wise"

Walter Chalmers Smith was one of a considerable number of 19th century Scottish intellectuals who devoted their lives to theology. He was also a minister of the Free Church, who reached the pinnacle of his profession. But he is best known as the author of a truly great hymn, "Immortal, invisible, God only wise."

He was educated at Aberdeen Grammar School and progressed to the university in that city. Wishing to further his theological studies he moved on to New College, Edinburgh, ultimately achieving a doctorate in Divinity. In 1850, when he was 26, he was ordained pastor of the Scottish Church in Chadwell Street, Islington.

He moved back to Scotland and was minister of Free Churches in Milnathort, near Kinross, and also in Glasgow before being appointed to the pastorate of the Free High Church in Edinburgh in 1876. This was one of the most prestigious appointments in the Free Church.

By then he had established himself as a very able poet, his poetry being a mixture of secular and sacred verse. In anthologies of Scottish poetry the reader may come across 'The Bishop's Walk', 'Olrig Grange' (named after a remote abode near Thurso on the Pentland Firth), 'Hilda among the Broken Gods' or 'North Country Folk'.

In 1876, the same year that he was appointed to the Free High Church in Edinburgh, Walter Chalmers Smith published his 'Hymns of Christ and Christian Life'. From this collection, 'Congregational Hymns' included four in its 1884 edition, thus bringing them to public notice. Of these, the most memorable was "Immortal, invisible, God only wise."

Dr. John Julian, in his 'Dictionary of Hymnology', describes Dr. Smith's hymns as being "rich in thought and vigorous in expression. They deserve and probably will receive greater notice than hitherto at the hands of hymnal compilers."

He was absolutely right. "Immortal, invisible" has become a tremendously popular hymn. It certainly is deep in tone, for a different theme of theological thought strikes one every time we read it. The phraseology and imagery are also striking, for such phrases as "the Ancient of Days", "silent as light" and "Thy justice like mountains" need no small amount of contemplation.

In fact, light is a recurrent theme of the hymn, and is mentioned four times. Arthur Temple reminds us that the French painter Gauguin died inconsolable because he was never able to paint light, and suggests that he would have been less despondent had he read the line "In light inaccessible hid from our eyes."

Perhaps Walter Chalmers Smith, coming from Aberdeen where the light glistens on the granite buildings after rain, turning them almost to silver, had an enhanced sense of light. Also the city is sufficiently far north to benefit from the Northern Lights in summer, when the daylight hardly ever disappears and the sunsets are breathtakingly radiant.

For a good part of the 20th century "Immortal, invisible" was a fixture in the top 20 of people's favourite hymns, both in Britain and Australia. It is a particular favourite of the Queen, who often requests it on commemorative occasions. A good deal of the hymn's popularity is due to the soaring, melodious tune 'St. Denio', or 'Joanna' as it is sometimes called. This is based on a Welsh folk song which was first used as a hymn tune in a Welsh hymnal published in 1839.

In 1893 Walter Chalmers Smith accepted the top post in his Church, Moderator of the Free Church of Scotland. This was four years after the death of a previous incumbent in that post, Horatius Bonar. He wrote literally hundreds of hymns, sometimes jotted down while waiting for a tram, so perhaps the two men spent their lunch hours at Convocation discussing the best hymn for the Epiphany.

Walter Chalmers Smith died in 1908, by then an old man of 84, but his great hymn "Immortal, invisible, God only wise" will ensure that his name will never be forgotten.

LOVE MARIA WILLIS
"Father, hear the prayer we offer"

Maria Willis was born in 1824 at Hancock on the Delaware River in New England, some 120 miles as the crow flies up country from New York. Her maiden name was Whitcomb. She married Frederick Willis, a doctor, in 1858 when she was 34, and they lived at Rochester, a sizeable town on the southern shores of Lake Ontario. For the later years of her long life (she lived to be 84) she moved a short distance southwards to Glenora, on Seneca Lake.

Her famous hymn was originally published in 1859, the year after she married, under the first line "Father, hear the prayer I offer." It appeared in 'Tiffany's Monthly', and after Maria revised it, it was published widely in both America and Britain. One of the changes she made was to substitute 'I' in the first line for 'we'. This is how it appeared in the 'English Hymnal' in 1906.

Maria was a Unitarian, and in 1864 it found a place in their hymnal, 'Hymns of the Spirit', edited by Samuel Johnson and Samuel Longfellow. Samuel Johnson was a radical and an ardent anti-slavery campaigner, who established his own Free Church at Lynn in Massachusetts. Longfellow was a brother of the poet Henry Longfellow and a friend of Samuel Johnson. Both men were more in tune with the Unitarians than any other sect.

Maria's single hymn, "Father, hear the prayer we offer," is a Christian's supplication for strength and courage to achieve something rather more in life than "the daily round, the common task." She wrote it in her mid-30s, still young enough to wish for some enterprise or even adventure in the Christian cause. The final verse is a very human plea for Divine protection through the unknown tribulations that may await us:

> "Be our strength in hours of weakness,
> In our wanderings be our Guide;
> Through endeavour, failure, danger,
> Father, be thou at our side."

The hymn has been criticised as an inaccurate representation of the 23rd Psalm, and one commentator, Erik Routley, describes it as 'banal'. But to the ordinary Sunday worshipper, seeking no particular intellectual or theological focus from a hymn, it is a comfort and a treasure, from a sincere and unremarkable Christian.

It is normally sung to the tune 'Sussex', which was adapted from a traditional English folk song by Ralph Vaughan Williams, composer of 'The Lark Ascending' and a great deal else. Several folk tunes were adapted by him for 'The English Hymnal', of which he was musical editor.

Maria Willis was one of several New England hymn-writers, all born within twenty years of her early in the 19th century. John Greenleaf Whittier wrote "Dear Lord and Father of mankind," Phillips Brooks "O little town of Bethlehem," Philipp Bliss scores of hymns for 'Sacred Songs and Solos', Julia Ward Howe "Mine eyes have seen the glory of the coming of the Lord" and Edmund Sears "It came upon the midnight clear." The last two, like Maria Willis, were Unitarians.

Maria died at Glenora in 1908. She would have been amazed to hear that a hundred years later her hymn is still a favourite on both sides of the Atlantic.

HARRIET PARR
"Hear my prayer, O Heavenly Father"

Harriet Parr was born in York in 1828 and grew up with an ardent desire to write. As women were not meant to depict the raw passions of love, hate, deceit and similar ingredients to be found in a good novel, she had the same problem as the Bronte sisters, living and writing not far away at Haworth, near Bradford. Harriet used the same device as the Brontes to overcome this Victorian reticence – she took a pen-name with a masculine ring to it.

Calling herself Holme Lee, she wrote 'Maude Talbot' when she was 26, and followed this over the next decade with a succession of other novels, all depicting the dramatic and romantic escapades of various young ladies. They included 'Sylvan Holt's Daughter', 'Warp and Woof', 'Mr. Wynyard's Ward' and 'Title of Honour'.

'Title of Honour' tells the tragic story of the romance between the Rev'd. Francis Gwynne (alias Henry Martyn) and Miss Eleanour Trevelyan (alias Lydia Grenfell). Harriet sticks to absolute historical accuracy, so the book has to end with the hero's lonely death in prison, which is guaranteed to send her readers to bed in a state of abject depression.

Her incursion into hymn-writing came in 1856 when she was 28. Charles Dickens published in the Christmas edition of 'Household Words', the magazine that he edited, her story entitled 'The Wreck of the Golden Mary', which contained her beautiful hymn "Hear my prayer, O Heavenly Father."

The story recounts how the 'Golden Mary' was on its way to California when it was struck by an iceberg in the Atlantic. At once it listed alarmingly as water gushed in. The order to abandon ship was given, and the passengers and crew took to the lifeboats only just in time, for the ship sunk as they gazed on in horror from the Atlantic waves.

For several days passengers and crew huddled in their lifeboats in a piteous state. Food and water were almost exhausted, they were wet through and the chances of anyone rescuing them in that watery world of vastness looked remote indeed. To keep their spirits up, the survivors decided to take turns at telling a story.

One of the occupants of the lifeboat featured in the story was a wild, fearless youth named Dick Tarrant. When it came to his turn, he said:

"What can it be that brings all these old things over my mind? There's a child's hymn I and Tom used to say at my mother's knee, when we were little ones, keeps running through my thoughts. It's the stars, maybe. There was a little window by my bed that I used to watch them at, a window in my room at home in Cheshire; and if I were ever afraid, as boys will be after reading a good ghost story, I would keep on saying it till I fell asleep."

One of his fellow survivors interjected, "That was a good mother of yours, Dick; could you say that hymn now, do you think? Some of us might like to hear it."

"It is as clear in my mind at this minute," replied Dick, "as if my mother was here listening to me." And he repeated:

> "Hear my prayer, O Heavenly Father,
>   Ere we lay us down to sleep;
>   Bid thine angels, pure and holy,
>   Round our bed their vigils keep."

And there, I am afraid, the story must end. I can find no record of the rest of the hymn, nor can I tell you what was the fate of those poor souls tossing on the Atlantic waves. But some of them must have survived, or we would have no account of Dick and his hymn. If anyone comes across the 1856 Christmas edition of 'Household Words' or the 'New Congregational Hymn Book' of 1859, in which the hymn is No. 945, they will be able to complete both hymn and story.

As for Harriet Parr, she continued writing for most of her life, her vivid imagination never failing to depict the adventures of heroines in dramatic circumstances. The Victorian periodicals fulfilled the public craving which in this day and age is satisfied by the television soap operas, and there were plenty of them.

Harriet lived to be 72, and died at the Isle of Wight coastal resort of Shanklin in 1900. Sad to relate, she never wrote another hymn.

ELLEN H. GATES
"I will sing you a song of that beautiful land"

Ellen Gates lived at a time when mission songs and hymns had a huge appeal, particularly in the USA where she lived. She was a contemporary of Fanny Crosby, who wrote 8,000 of them although totally blind from infancy, and the two ladies lived not far apart in the New York area.

Ellen's maiden name was Huntington, and she was born early in the 19th century at Torrington in Connecticut, some 80 miles as the crow flies north east of New York. The family moved to Elizabeth in New Jersey, much closer to the great metropolis, and her name became known in the mission field when she started to contribute hymns and gospel songs to American mission and Sunday school hymnals.

Ira Sankey, ever on the look-out for a poignant sacred poem for Moody's revivalist meetings, included several of her pieces in 'Sacred Songs and Solos', which immediately popularised them to the American public. They became popular in Britain as well, when the two great revivalists extended their activities to this side of the Atlantic.

Their hymnal included two of her best loved hymns, "I will sing you a song of that beautiful land" and "If you cannot on the ocean." Ellen married Isaac Gates, and they lived in New York for most of their lives. She had the gift of writing for children as well as adults, and her simple, poignant words were immensely appealing. They even reduced America's most famous president to tears.

She said of her hymn "If you cannot on the ocean," which was written as a poem but used as a hymn in America, "The lines were written upon my slate one snowy afternoon in the winter of 1860. I knew, as I know now, that the poem was only a simple little thing, but somehow I had a presentiment that it had wings, and would fly into sorrowful hearts, uplifting and strengthening them."

President Lincoln was present in the Hall of Representatives in Washington in 1865 when the famous gospel singer Philip Phillips sang this hymn. The President was moved to tears by the touching poem and its melody, and wrote a note to the Chairman of the meeting, the Hon. William H. Seward. It stated, "Near the end, let us have 'Your Mission' (the title of the hymn) repeated by Mr. Phillips. Don't say I called for it. A. Lincoln." The President had his wish, but not his anonymity, and it became known throughout America that this was Abraham Lincoln's favourite hymn!

Philip Phillips worked with Ellen Gates from time to time on mission songs. On one occasion in 1865 he needed a good funeral hymn that would really bring comfort to the bereaved, so he wrote to Mrs. Gates and asked her to attempt the task. To aid her he enclosed the following extract from 'Pilgrim's Progress', in which John Bunyan gives his readers a glimpse of his idea of heaven:

"Now I saw in my dream that these two men went in at the gate; and lo, as they entered, they were transfigured; and they had raiment put on them that shone like gold. There were also those that met them with harps and crowns, and gave to them; the harps to praise withal, and the crowns in token of honour. Then I heard in my dream that all the bells in the city rang again for joy, and that it was said unto them: 'Enter ye into the joy of your Lord!' Now, just as the gates were opened to let in the men, I looked in after them, and behold the city shone like the sun; the streets also were paved with gold; and in them walked many men, with crowns on their heads and palms in their hands, and golden harps to sing praises withal. After that, they shut up the gates, which, when I had seen, I wished myself among them."

Ellen was also captivated by Bunyan's imagery, and sent back her new hymn. It began:

"I will sing you a song of that beautiful land,
 The far-away home of the soul;
Where no storms ever beat on the glittering strand,
 While the years of eternity roll."

Mr. Phillips was at once smitten by her verses, and abandoning all his plans for the day he read again John Bunyan's memorable words, which come at the end of his great book. He then sat down at his organ, put his little boy on his knee and started to play.

The tune that resulted seemed to come more by divine inspiration than by human effort, and in that rather sentimental age words and melody gave immeasurable comfort to grieving souls. One man told him years later that he had sung it at 120 funerals, and Philip Phillips added the poignant footnote: "It was sung at the funeral of my own dear boy, who had sat on my knee when I wrote the tune."

As for Ellen Gates and her husband Isaac, they spent their latter years in New York, watching their city expand outwards and upwards. Ellen wrote a number of other hymns, but none that equalled the popularity of her Bunyan inspired glimpse of heaven.

ELIZABETH C. CLEPHANE
"Beneath the Cross of Jesus"

In Volume 2 of this series I related a story that occurred during the first mission to Britain by the great American evangelists Moody and Sankey in 1874. They embarked on a train at Glasgow to move on to a four month mission to Edinburgh, and Sankey, who was the musician and solo singer of the partnership, bought a newspaper for the journey. He wanted to see if it contained any news of what was happening back home in America.

He found no American news to interest him, but a poem at the bottom of an inside page caught his attention. "Listen to this," he said to his companion, and proceeded to read the first verse:

> "There were ninety and nine that safely lay
> In the shelter of the fold;
> But one was out on the hills away,
> Far off from the gates of gold;
> Away on the mountains, wild and bare,
> Away from the tender Shepherd's care."

But Moody only grunted, for his attention was engrossed in his sermon notes for that evening's mission meeting. So Sankey cut out the poem and stuck it into his music notebook which he always carried with him.

On the second day of their Edinburgh mission, Moody preached with great fervour on the subject 'The Good Shepherd'. He then called upon Dr. Horatius Bonar to give a brief address. Dr. Bonar was minister of the popular Chambers Memorial Free Church in Edinburgh, and was not only a great theological scholar but also a prolific evangelical hymn-writer.

While Dr. Bonar was speaking, Moody tiptoed over to Ira D. Sankey at the organ and whispered to him to try and find a hymn relevant to his Good Shepherd theme. Sankey searched his music but could find nothing appropriate. Then he remembered the poem he had cut out on the train. He just had time to fish it out of his music notebook and place it on the organ rest when Dr. Bonar finished his address.

Sankey then took a remarkably brave decision. As he was called upon to sing, he decided that he would try to compose a tune for the sacred poem on the spur of the moment, and sing it to a congregation of over a thousand people. Not only did he achieve this, but his melody proved an absolute masterpiece.

As he came to the second verse a fresh difficulty confronted him. Could he manage to remember the tune that he had just composed on the spur of the moment? This also he achieved, and as tears streamed down the faces of his audience who had burst into thunderous applause, Dwight Moody came over to him again.

"Where did you get that hymn?" he asked in amazement. "I never heard the like of it in my life!"

"Why, it is the hymn I read to you on the train two days ago," replied Sankey, beaming with divine inspiration.

The poem was written by Elizabeth Clephane, whose death had occurred five years previously, aged only 39. She was born in Edinburgh in 1830 but her family moved to the lovely border town of Melrose when she was still very young. Perhaps her literary inclination was influenced by the proximity of her home to Sir Walter Scott's Abbotsford, which was only three miles away.

The Clephane family consisted of her father who was a sheriff of the county court, her mother who was a member of the famous Douglas clan, and three daughters. They were ardent Presbyterians, and were well known in the town for their good works towards the poor and destitute. Although not particularly well off themselves, they never refused to give what they could to a deserving cause.

Elizabeth was always frail as a child and troubled repeatedly by illness, but she had a perpetual smile on her pretty face. She was too shy to say much to the townsfolk who came to her home or met her in the street, but because of her good nature and cheery disposition she was known universally as Sunbeam.

Most of her poetry was religious in tone, and much of it was published in 'The Family Treasury', a Presbyterian journal. But a good deal of it was published posthumously, and she would be amazed to hear that people are still singing today the words she wrote. "Beneath the cross of Jesus" first appeared in 'The Family Treasury' in 1872, three years after her death.

It is a very devout, sincere hymn, rather personal in tone and hence suitable for private devotions. It is clearly the work of a deeply committed Christian, who prized salvation as one of the great blessings of her life. In its original form it has five verses, and it is so good that it is a shame many hymnals today have shortened it. The original fourth verse reads:

"Upon that Cross of Jesus
Mine eye at times can see
The very dying form of One
Who suffered there for me.
And from my smitten heart, with tears,
Two wonders I confess –
The wonder of his glorious love,
And my own worthlessness."

Ira D. Sankey composed his own tune for the hymn in the house of Dr. Barnardo, the founder of the homes for outcast children. The following morning he sang the hymn to a packed congregation at the mission service in the Bow Road Hall, in London's East End. Moody was preaching elsewhere on that occasion, and the preacher was The Rev'd. W Hay MH Aitken, a renowned mission speaker.

When Sankey finished his solo most of the congregation were wiping tears from their eyes, including Mr. Aitken. He told the packed hall that he had intended to preach to them on the subject of Christian work, but as they were all so moved by the hymn he would speak instead on 'The Cross of Jesus'.

He proceeded to preach such a powerful sermon, delivered of course without a single note, that his flock trooped out into the morning sunshine stunned and elated. Some claimed to remember his words years later. The hymn came to be particularly popular in Canada and Australia.

Another tune sometimes used for the hymn is 'St. Christopher', composed by Frederick Charles Maker. He was an organist at Nonconformist churches in Bristol. A much older melody that some hymnals used to prefer is 'Helder', written by Bartholomaeus Helder, who died in 1635.

FRANCIS POTT
"Angel voices ever singing"

Francis Pott was another of those Victorian clerics who dedicated their lives to their flocks in English villages, the one member of the community who could bridge the social divide between the landed gentry and the villagers. Although, perhaps, rather too studious for the simple intellects of most of his parishoners, he was always respected and held in affection by those who came to him for spiritual or more practical guidance.

On the desk of his rectory study, probably weighed down by a hefty paperweight to stop it wafting away in the perpetual draught that found its way through the French windows, there would normally be the manuscript of a hymn. He wrote several original ones, including "Angel voices ever singing", and the Ascension Day favourite, "Lift up your heads, eternal gates." "Forty days and forty nights" is at least in part attributed to him.

He also translated many others, including "The strife is o'er, the battle done." It comes from a Latin hymn, possibly written in the 12th century. Most of Pott's hymns were published in his 'Hymns fitted to the Order of Common Prayer', published when he was 29. He was so well thought of by his contemporary hymnologists that he was invited to be on the committee that compiled the original 'Hymns Ancient and Modern'.

"Angel voices ever singing" is a gladsome hymn of praise. It is an absolute joy to sing, partly because the imagery of angels plucking harps and craftsmen creating beautiful things is so exuberant. Verse 2 is positively exciting, with the idea that God in all his majesty will stop to listen to the paltry words of praise of mere humans like us. Its climax in the final line fully justifies its two exclamation marks:

> "Thou, who art beyond the farthest
> Mortal eye can scan,
> Can it be that Thou regardest
> Songs of sinful man?

Can we know that Thou art near us,
And wilt hear us?
Yea! We can!"

The other joy of this hymn is the wonderfully cheering tune 'Angel Voices' composed by Dr. E.G. Monk, who was a contemporary of Francis Pott. It leaves one feeling happy and elated for having sung it, and is as near as we humans can get to offering an acceptable anthem of praise to the Almighty.

Other tunes that can be used are another melody called 'Angel Voices' by Sir Arthur Sullivan, and 'Seraphim' by Samuel Sebastian Wesley, illegitimate son of Samuel Wesley who was the nephew of John, the founder of the Methodist Church. The hymn is often sung on All Saints' Day.

Francis Pott was born in 1832 and educated at Brasenose College, Oxford. He graduated in 1854 and was ordained two years later. For ten years he was a curate, but in those days when pluralities were not uncommon, curates often had sole charge of their parishes and were sometimes rarely visited by their incumbents.

His first curacy was at Bishopsworth, which today is a southern suburb of Bristol. He then moved to Ardingly, situated on the Sussex downs overlooking the valley of the Ouse. In due course he moved 25 miles or so further east to the attractive village of Ticehurst, standing amidst rolling hills with views across the Rother. The broach spire of his church there was (and still is) a local landmark.

In 1866, when he was 34, he was appointed rector of Northill in Bedfordshire, a village not far from Biggleswade in flat country, mainly used for growing vegetables. There he remained for the rest of his ministry. As he approached 60 increasing deafness caused him to resign his living.

He spent his retirement at Speldhurst, a village near Tunbridge Wells, so returning to the undulating area of hills, valleys and peaceful villages that he had enjoyed so much when a curate. He died in 1909 aged 77, and in the village churches his hymns of praise and joy still linger on the tranquil air of a Sunday morning. The angel voices continue to sing.

SAMUEL FILLMORE BENNETT
"There's a land that is fairer than day"

One day in the mid-19th century Samuel Bennett sat in his office in the small Wisconsin town of Elkhorn, working at his desk. In came a musician friend of his, Joseph P. Webster, who merely grunted in reply to Bennett's greeting. He looked thoroughly depressed with life.

His friend asked him what was the matter, but he clearly was not in the mood for conversation and simply murmured something about "It would be all right by and by." Webster then made for the fire and huddled there. Samuel Bennett was used to his friend's fits of melancholy, and had found in the past that the best way to change his mood was to get him to compose a tune.

Bennett's interest had been aroused by his friend's casual remark, and he seized on the final phrase with enthusiasm.

"The sweet by and by," he mused. "Would that not make a good hymn?" Webster muttered that it might, and showed by his general demeanour that he was not interested in debating the point.

Samuel Bennett then pushed aside his work, and seizing a sheet of paper he wrote as fast as his hand could manage it the three verses and chorus of what was to become a gospel song that was sung throughout the world:

> "There's a land that is fairer than day,
> And by faith we can see it afar,
> For the Father waits over the way,
> To prepare us a dwelling-place there.
>
> *In the sweet by and by*
> *We shall meet on that beautiful shore.*
>
> We shall sing on that beautiful shore
> The melodious songs of the blest;

And our spirits shall sorrow no more –
Not a sigh for the blessing of rest.

To our bountiful Father above
We will offer the tribute of praise,
For the glorious gift of his love,
And the blessings that hallow our days."

Bennett handed his work to his depressed musician friend, who read it through. He immediately snapped out of his depression and in turn seated himself at the desk. Equally rapidly, Webster started to write a melody for the words, and within 30 minutes of first arriving in the office, he had composed a tune for the hymn. He had even produced four parts for the chorus, as well.

Meanwhile three other friends had entered the office, which was obviously a favourite meeting place for Bennett's evangelical friends. One of them had a violin with him, and on that instrument Webster played over his tune.

"That hymn is immortal!" exclaimed one of the bystanders, and indeed his words were to prove prophetic. Sankey included it in his mission hymnal 'Sacred Songs and Solos', and the Salvation Army took it up with great ardour. It was particularly popular at funeral services, but at a time when life was hard and spirits really did sorrow, it struck a chord of certain hope in the life hereafter.

It is a remarkable fact that within 30 minutes of Webster making his remark "It will be all right by and by," both words and music were completed and the five men were standing there singing the hymn to the accompaniment of a violin.

It is all very well to decry gospel songs as inferior verse full of sentimental imagery sung to pop music, but the fact is they appealed to hundreds of thousands of people. They were unsophisticated souls seeking for something to give them some hope and joy as they lived out their poverty-riven existences, and the revivalist music was a major factor in bringing faith to the masses. Samuel Bennett and his friends produced a hymn that gave joy to countless numbers of people.

Bennett was an active evangelist all his life in an age when evangelism was rampant, particularly in the USA. This was epitomised by the stirring missions of Moody and Sankey. He died in 1898, aged 62.

FOLLIOT SANDFORD PIERPOINT
"For the beauty of the earth"

Folliot Sandford Pierpoint was fortunate enough to be born and to grow up in Bath, a town full of glorious buildings set in a most beautiful location, with hills rising up all around it. Even today it is a dramatic experience approaching the city, and in his time it was far more so, with the spires and crescents beckoning the slow progress onwards in that horse and cart age.

He wrote a number of hymns, most of which were overlooked by the predominantly evangelical hymnals of his day as they were too Anglo Catholic for their tastes. There are frequent references to the sacrament, the chalice and the Virgin Mary, all rather provocative to an age that was easily provoked by anything with leanings towards Rome.

But one of his hymns, "For the beauty of the earth," is still very popular today, and is a simple thanksgiving for the beauty of the world around us and the love of God that enfolds us. It details the earth, the skies, hill and vale, tree and flower, sun and moon and stars of light.

Its author was clearly a man who appreciated his Somerset home, and who had the soul of a true poet. Folliot Pierpoint was born at Bathwick in Bath two years before Queen Victoria succeeded to the throne.

He was the youngest son of William Pierpoint, a gentleman wealthy enough not to need a profession. He inherited family property and married Annabella Sandford, a well endowed Shropshire girl eighteen years younger than he was. Her family owned land adjoining the River Severn, north of Shrewsbury.

Both his elder brothers became clergymen, Richard at Eastbourne and Edward a schoolmaster clergyman who taught first at Sheffield Grammar

BATH as it was in Folliot Pierpoint's youth:
Market Place and Guildhall

School and later in Bath. Folliot was educated at King Edward's Grammar School in Bath, and from there progressed to Queen's College, Cambridge. In those days this was a strongly evangelical college, but Folliot was far more interested in the Oxford Movement, which was then all the rage at that rival establishment.

The Church of England was going through a time of laxity, with pluralities rife and many ordained clergymen without any sincere sense of vocation. A plurality was the practice whereby a clergyman could hold two or more incumbencies concurrently, sometimes hardly bothering to set foot in some of their less appealing parishes.

Younger sons of the landed gentry, who had no land to inherit, opted for second best and took a country living, where their rectories were often large houses with plenty of land, sometimes even with fishing and shooting rights. The lifestyle was good, but most had no vocation to the priesthood.

It was to put a stop to these practices and to assert the authority and dignity of the Anglican Church that was the basis of the Oxford Movement, and Pierpoint was an enthusiastic apostle. But he was never ordained, instead joining the staff of Somersetshire College in Bath to teach Classics. This school had recently been founded to provide a secondary education to boys along public school lines.

After twenty years there he moved on to teach at a school in Devonport, where his pupils included Percival Wren. He was the author of the novel 'Beau Geste' which was a racy best-seller in its day. When the school in Devonport closed he attempted unsuccessfully to start one of his own. He ended his teaching career in Deptford, teaching trainee students for his own career.

In retirement he settled first on the Isle of Wight and then at Newport in South Wales, which was his home at the time of his death in 1917. During his life he published three volumes of poems and his hymns, of which "For the beauty of the earth" is the only one to survive.

He wrote it when he was still an undergraduate, after returning from a ramble in the hills near Bath, but it was not published until eleven years had elapsed.

Then it was included by the Rev'd. Orby Shipley in his 'Lyra Eucharistica' as a communion hymn, and the compilers of 'Hymns Ancient and Modern' amended it slightly to make it suitable as a general hymn and not simply a Eucharistic one.

It has been sung over the years to all kinds of different tunes, including 'Dix' composed by Conrad Kocher and better known as the tune for "As with gladness, men of old." Henry Smart came up with 'Heathlands' which had its adherents, but probably the favourite with most people is 'England's Lane', an adaptation by Geoffrey Shaw of an Elizabethan folk song.

ARTHUR CAMPBELL AINGER
"God is working his purpose out"

Arthur Campbell Ainger was born in 1841 in London. His father Thomas was vicar of Hampstead and a Prebendary of St. Paul's Cathedral. Arthur was sent to Eton, where he proved a gifted pupil who excelled in the Classics. He became engrossed in all that Britain's leading public school had to offer, and was destined to spend not only his schooldays but also his entire working career of 37 years there.

He moved on to Trinity College, Cambridge, where he achieved a First in Classics. Although he probably never realised it at the time, he was one of a number of Trinity College graduates who went on to become well-known hymn-writers. The list includes John Ellerton, Sir Henry Williams Baker, John Byrom, George Herbert, Christopher Wordsworth and Henry Alford, to name but six.

Ainger's best-known hymn is the wonderfully exciting "God is working his purpose out," which is an illustration of the lines in the Lord's Prayer: "Thy kingdom come, thy will be done, on earth as it is in heaven." The supreme message of confidence that the hymn inspires reaches a triumphant climax at the end of the final verse, with the words:

"Yet ever nearer draws the time, the time that shall surely be,
When the earth shall be filled with the glory of God, as the waters cover
the sea."

The last two lines of each verse are taken from Isaiah 11, verse 9.

The hymn is normally sung to the tune 'Benson', so called because Ainger dedicated the hymn to Archbishop Benson, a former public school headmaster. The tune has a strong harmony that builds up a crescendo as it progresses, so that the final lines have a triumphant ring about them. It is a fine tune for a large, enthusiastic congregation to sing, immensely satisfying for hundreds of public school boys all eager to participate in the emotion of the occasion. It was composed specially for the hymn by Millicent Kingham, a church organist from Hertford. The hymn is also sometimes sung to the tune 'Purpose', composed by Arthur Shaw.

Two other hymns by Arthur Ainger are still to be found in most hymnals, "Let all God's people join in one" and "God of our fathers, unto thee." He wrote his hymns primarily for the use of Eton College, and when in a more secular mood turned his hand to school songs. He wrote the Founder's Day Hymn for King Henry VI, starting:

> "Praise the Lord! Today we sing,
> Birthday of our founder King!"

He had the onerous task of keeping up with Harrow, which has a unique tradition of excellence in this respect.

Ainger first became a Classics master at Eton in 1864 at the age of 23, and he remained there for 37 years until he retired in 1901. A heartfelt tribute to his career as an Eton schoolmaster is contained in the 'Handbook of Revised Church Hymnary', written by an unknown source but probably a colleague:

"He was one of the most distinguished and useful of Eton masters, a man of clear head, controlling character, wide accomplishments, a fine and habile scholar of the old school, with a remarkable memory, an incisive speaker, a good critic, fertile in suggestion, complete in execution. He preserved admirable and friendly discipline by means of a dry and ready irony, which was never harsh or unamiable. He set no punishments, and his justice, courtesy and unruffled good humour won him the respect and admiration of the boys."

Ainger's abiding interests were in the Classics and the history of Eton. He wrote a book of reminiscences about the school as well as a Latin verse dictionary and a book about the game of fives.

He would just have overlapped at Eton, by about eighteen months, with a young master called Cyril Alington, who was described as "The most alive and brilliant of the younger masters – the best preacher, the most entertaining division master, the most inspiring tutor." Alington was also a hymn-writer (featured in Volume 2), and it would be tempting if fanciful to picture them in some corner of the masters' common-room during break, smoking their pipes and discussing animatedly the best hymns for Ascension Day!

Alington became Headmaster of Shrewsbury in 1917, two years before Ainger's death. Later he was appointed Head Master of Eton. His hymns include "Lord of beauty, thine the splendour" and the Easter hymn, "Good Christian men, rejoice and sing."

Arthur Ainger died in 1919, aged 78.

WILLIAM H.M.H. AITKEN
"O leave we all for Jesus"

William Aitken was the youngest son of the Rev'd. Robert Aitken, the incumbent of Pendeen, a village on the westerly tip of Cornwall. Many of his parishioners there worked in the tin mines. William was born in 1841 and educated at Wadham College, Oxford, graduating in 1865.

William Pennefather, featured earlier in this volume, heard of the young man's enthusiasm for mission work, and while on holiday in the West Country he made the journey to Pendeen to explore the possibility of young William joining him at Mildmay Park, north London, as a curate. In fact, William was not yet ordained, but he had made the decision to follow his father into Holy Orders. Before Pennefather left Cornwall, he offered William the curacy.

Robert Aitken advised his youngest son to accept the post at St. Jude's, Mildmay Park. "I think you will do wisely in going to Mildmay," he said. "True, Mr. Pennefather is a very Low Churchman, and you may meet with many other men whose views may more fully coincide with your own; but I feel sure that Mr. Pennefather is a very holy man, and that's the great point – and you won't get that everywhere."

The advice was fully borne out by the five years William spent at Mildmay, eighteen months of which were spent living with the Pennefathers at the parsonage. The couple felt with typical kindness that the culture shock for a young man from rural Cornwall moving to north London would be daunting, and a Christian home environment would be a lot more pleasant for him than an anonymous lodging-house.

Pennefather was decidedly Evangelical in his outlook whereas William shared his father's High Church proclivities, but this did not count with Pennefather in his choice of a young curate. It did lead to some criticism from St. Jude's parishioners, but Pennefather always shielded William from adverse remarks. As William later wrote, "His kindness and tender affection to me from the first were something wonderful, yet I hardly remember any other peron ever speaking to me with such plainness of what he considered to be my faults."

While at Mildmay, William Aitken married a local girl, and shortly afterwards, in 1871, was presented to the living of Christ Church, Everton, in Liverpool. This was a city with huge mission potential at that time.

On one occasion he had a large number of confirmation candidates whom he was busy preparing, which occupied much of his time. But he received an urgent call from his father, who had moved on to Newport, to come and help out at a big mission gathering he was conducting in his parish of St. Paul's. He had to go, although he was very reluctant to leave his own pressing parochial affairs.

On reaching Newport, he found that his father was insistent upon him preaching at the Sunday evening service. William felt that his father's words would have been far more stirring than his own to the huge congregation, but he duly took his place in the pulpit and delivered the sermon.

That night he found that the pressures of the mission and his worries regarding his own confirmation candidates back in Liverpool made sleep impossible. After tossing and turning for an hour or two he finally gave up the attempt, rose from his bed, lit the lamp on the bedside table and composed a hymn that was sung at the confirmation service in his own parish.

The first verse reads:
> "O leave we all for Jesus –
> The world that fades away,

117

The flesh with its wild passions,
And Satan's tyrant sway;
We leave it all for Jesus,
Nor will we count it loss;
For who the fine gold gaining,
Will grudge to lose the dross?"

The hymn was later published in the 'Church Parochial Mission Book', a hymnal of which William Aitken was the editor. He was always on the look-out for an original edition to its pages, and one came his way in a strange and rather charming manner.

A mother and her eight-year-old daughter were returning home from an evangelistic meeting, at which the hymn "Knocking, knocking, who is there?" had been sung. The little girl was unusually pensive, and when asked why, she said she was worried by the final verse, which concludes:

"Yes, the pierced hand still knocketh,
And beneath the crowned hair
Beam the patient eyes, so tender,
Of thy Saviour waiting there."

"I don't think the hymn ought to end like that," said the little girl to her mother, "because, you see, it leaves the Saviour still standing outside."

Her mother thought no more of it, but when they reached home, her daughter went up to her room and remained there some time. When she finally emerged she was clutching a piece of paper. "I think it should finish something like this," she said, and handed her mother the sheet of paper. On it was written, in neat, rounded script:

"Enter, enter, Heavenly Guest!
Welcome! Welcome to my breast!
I have long withstood thy knocking,
For my heart was full of sin;
But thy love hath overcome me,
Blessed Jesus – O come in!"

The mother was very impressed with her daughter's literary efforts, and also by the theology behind the words. So proud was she that she sent off the verse to a religious periodical, with an account of who wrote it and why. The magazine printed it, and so it was seen by William Aitken, who added the final verse to the existing hymn in the 'Church Parochial Mission Hymn Book'.

William Aitken resigned his living at Christ Church, Everton, in 1875, after four years in Liverpool, in order to devote himself entirely to parochial mission work. This involved sometimes quite lengthy stays in parishes that had invited him to conduct missions. We can trace some of his itinerary from where his hymns were written, places that included Derby, Bedford and Southampton.

He often found himself addressing huge crowds, most of whom were not regular churchgoers. Sometimes he managed to win souls for Christ, sometimes his words fell on deaf ears. In 1877 he was appointed general superintendent of the Church Parochial Mission Society, and in the 1870s he edited two editions of 'Hymns for a Parochial Mission'. He also composed 24 tunes for that hymnal.

He tells the story of one rich and fashionable young lady who attended one of his missions in the West End of London. He pleaded with the congregation to let Christ enter their lives, but this young lady was completely unmoved, and made for the doors as soon as the sermon was over.

As she pushed and squeezed her way down the aisle, which was a slow business, she became engrossed by the words of Mrs. Codner's hymn, "Lord, I hear of showers of blessing." It is a very personal hymn, with frequent use of the personal pronoun, and it is set to an appealing tune by W.H. Bradbury. It was a popular hymn late in the 19th century, and appears in Moody and Sankey's hymnal, 'Sacred Songs and Solos'.

By the time the lady reached the door, the choir was singing the final verse:

"Pass me not, thy lost one bringing,
Bind my heart, O Lord, to thee!
While the streams of life are springing,

Norwich Cathedral Choristers with Dean and Chapter, 1913. William Hay Aitken is seated, 4th from left.

Blessing others, O bless me! Even me!"

As she walked home and tried to sleep that night, she could not get the words out of her mind. She felt that in her materialistic existence she was excluding a vital presence from her life, and the following evening she returned to the church to declare herself one of William Aitken's converts. Similar stories of strange instances of conversions were remarkably frequent in the days of the mission services.

In 1900 William Aitken was appointed a residential canon at Norwich Cathedral. He remained there for 27 years, during which time he graduated to Vice-Dean of the cathedral. There is a simple wall tablet to his memory in the south ambulatory, which refers to him as "mission preacher, canon and vice-dean." He died in 1927 at the age of 86.

ROBERT BRIDGES
"O sacred head, sore wounded"

Robert Bridges was a Victorian gentleman who had a passion for the beauty of the world, and for poetry. He retired to the countryside when still in his 30s, and devoted his long life to writing and improving the quality of English hymnody.

He was born in 1844 and educated at Eton and Corpus Christi, Oxford. He then studied medicine at St. Bartholomew's Hospital in London, and worked at the Children's Hospital in Great Ormond Street and the Great Northern Hospital. After eight years he retired from medicine in 1882 at the age of 38 and went to live in Berkshire, first at Boar's Hill and then at Yattendon.

Today the village is only a mile or so away from the M4, but in those days it was a deeply rural community where he could write with no distractions apart from the mooing of cows and the sound of early morning chaffinches. He became very attached to the place, and for many years was the village choir-master.

As a poet of outstanding technique and perfection of form, he became disillusioned at the feeble nature of many of the hymns he was required to present to his choir, so he determined to assemble his own hymnal, the 'Yattendon Hymnal'. This contained 100 new hymns, some translations from existing hymns and others his own composition. The latter category included "Rejoice, O land, in God thy might."

Perhaps his best known translation is "All my hope in God is founded," from Joachim Neander's 17th century "Meine Hoffnung stehet feste," which was originally intended to be used as a grace after meals. Neander wrote his own tune for the hymn, but a far more exciting tune is 'Michael', composed by Herbert Howells in response to a request from the director of music at

Charterhouse. Howells wrote the tune immediately after opening the letter requesting it, sitting at the breakfast table with his coffee getting cold.

"O sacred head, sore wounded" was originally written in Latin, probably in the 14th century. 300 years later the hymn was translated into German by a Lutheran pastor, Paul Gerhardt, who wrote well over 100 hymns.

Gerhardt lived through the troubled times of the Thirty Years' War in Germany, when his country was torn apart by religious bigotry. He spent the first 44 years of his life without a settled home, and suffered the trauma of losing his wife and children when still a young man. His was a lonely existence thereafter, and many of his hymns start with "I," which suggests that in writing them he found relief from his personal grief.

Several attempts at an English translation for "O sacred head" were made, including one by Sir Henry Williams Baker, the first editor of 'Hymns Ancient and Modern'. But the version printed in many hymnals today is by Robert Bridges, first appearing in the 'Yattendon Hymnal' in 1899. He translated it not from the German but from the original Latin.

The usual tune for the hymn is 'Passion Chorale', composed by Hans Leo Hassler 300 years before the translation by Bridges. Ian Bradley tells us that it was originally composed for a love song, but its slow, poignant notes are far more appropriate for Passion-tide devotions. Johann Sebastian Bach was particularly fond of the tune, and used it five times in his 'St. Matthew Passion'.

The words of Robert Bridges are an inspiring Good Friday contemplation in themselves, wonderfully spiritual and a personal devotion of great piety. The trauma of the Passion has inspired some fine hymnody over the centuries, Samuel Crossman's "My song is love unknown" and "When I survey the wondrous cross" from the pen of Isaac Watts being equally moving.

Robert Bridges uses the same personal pronoun as Gerhardt in his translation, which strikes a personal chord with the worshipper on that most holy occasion, Good Friday. The final verse reads:

"In thy most bitter passion
My heart to thee doth cry,
With thee for my salvation
Upon the cross to die.
Ah, keep my heart thus moved
To stand thy cross beneath,
To mourn thee, well-beloved,
Yet thank thee for thy death."

His poetry has an endearing serenity of expression and a stringent correctness about it. Perhaps Robert Bridges was too scholarly a person and his subjects too classical for him to attain a mass appeal, but he is generally regarded as the most artistic poet of his generation. This was officially endorsed in 1913 when he was appointed Poet Laureate.

His earlier volumes were printed privately, but in 1890 two volumes were published commercially. These were 'Shorter Poems' and 'Achilles in Scyros'. The following year 'Eden', his oratorio, was performed in Birmingham, which first brought him to the notice of the public. It is a noteworthy work, with the music composed by Stanford.

Other major works are 'Milton's Prosody', published in 1893, 'The Spirit of Man', 1916, and 'The Testament of Beauty', published in the final year of his life and considered a masterpiece. Bridges dedicated it to King George V.

Typical of the tranquility and technical perfection of his verse is his little poem 'Nightingales', with its deep reaches of contemplative reflection. The first verse goes:

"Beautiful must be the mountains where ye come,
And bright in the fruitful valleys the streams, where from

Ye learn your song:
Where are these starry woods? O might I wander there,
Among the flowers, which in that heavenly air
Bloom the year long!"

Robert Bridges lived to be an old man of 86. He died in 1930 and is buried at
Yattendon, that corner of Berkshire he loved so dearly.

WILLIAM St. HILL BOURNE
"The Sower went forth sowing"

When William St. Hill Bourne was a 28-year-old curate in charge of Christ Church, south Ashford, Kent, he wrote a hymn for their Harvest Festival service in 1874. It was simply printed on a sheet of paper for that single occasion. But someone in his congregation, largely composed of railway workers and their wives, was impressed enough with it to send it off to the religious periodical 'Church Bells', who published it.

From there it was spotted by the compilers of 'Hymns Ancient and Modern', who wanted to include it in their revised edition of 1875. But there was no obvious tune to go with it, so they wrote to Frederick Bridge, the organist at Westminster Abbey, (later Sir Frederick), beseeching him to compose a tune for it.

It so happened that the musician's little daughter Beatrice lay dying when he received the letter, and in his highly emotional state he was much moved by the third verse:

> "Within a hallowed acre
>   He sows yet other grain,
> When peaceful earth receiveth
>   The dead he died to gain;
> For though the growth be hidden,
>   We know that they shall rise;
> Yea, even now they ripen
>   In sunny paradise.
> O happy land of harvest,
>   O fields for ever white
> With souls that wear Christ's raiment,
>   With crowns of golden light!"

He sat down at his piano and composed a tune that surprised even himself, for he declared later that it was quite unlike any other tune that he had ever composed. He named it St. Beatrice in memory of his little girl, and both words and tune became inseparably linked for well over a century.

It was only later in the 20th century that the hymn lost its popularity, the sentimental nature of the words containing a somewhat Victorian theology. This is particularly true of the ending of the final verse:

> "O holy, awful Reaper,
> Have mercy in the day
> Thou puttest in thy sickle,
> And cast us not away."

Apart from Harvest Festivals, the hymn was also often sung at funerals. William St. Hill Bourne wrote a number of other hymns, often for specific church occasions. They were generally produced on fly-sheets for single occasions, and the author, being a modest man, never thought enough of them to gather them together into a collection. Two of the best were one written in praise of the new day, "For the freshness of the morning," and an evening hymn, "The evening shadowy dimness."

William St. Hill Bourne was born in 1846 and educated at Merchant Taylors' School and the London College of Divinity. After ordination in 1869 he acted as a curate in four different parishes in six years. He started at Holy Trinity, Derby, moved on to Harrow-on-the-Hill, from there to the Sussex coast at St. Leonard's-on-Sea and then to Ashford.

In 1875, at the age of 29, he was appointed perpetual curate of Pinner, which he would have known well from his time at Harrow. He was described as having "the duties of a vicar and the stipend of a curate." The old vicarage at Pinner was in such a dilapidated state that a maid's leg came through the ceiling.

He spent five years there and became well known in Evangelical circles from the verse he contributed to religious periodicals. One of his contributions, this time a prose work, was an article entitled 'Church Work and the Working Classes', which first appeared in 'Church Bells'.

While at Pinner he was invited to take on the editorship of 'The Mission Field', the magazine of the Society for the Propagation of the Gospel. All through his life he had a special interest in missionary work.

In 1880 he became vicar of All Saints, Haggerston, an East End parish that contained some of the worst slums in London. It should be remembered that at this time in our history, missionary work was every bit as relevant in the cramped courts and alleys of our own big cities as it was in Africa and India.

In 1900 he was appointed rector of Finchley where he proved a popular and successful incumbent of this important parish. He remained there for 24 years until his retirement in 1924. He died six years later at the age of 84.

SOMERSET CORRY LOWRY
"A Man there lived in Galilee"

Like William Pennefather and Thomas Kelly, both featured earlier in this volume, Somerset Lowry came from an Anglo-Irish legal family, but considerably after them. He was born in 1855 at Dungannon in Northern Ireland, although before the days of partition. His father, James Corry Lowry, was an eminent Q.C.

Somerset Lowry was sent over the water to Repton for his education, and from there went up to Trinity Hall, Cambridge. He graduated in 1877. Two years later he was ordained, and went as a curate to Doncaster.

He must have found the smoke and slums of south Yorkshire a different world to the small farms of Co. Armagh, but he remained there some time. It was a daunting start to his ministry for a young man with a public school background and no doubt it served him well in his future career.

In 1891 he was appointed to the living of North Holmwood, near Dorking in Surrey. His church of St. John's was only sixteen years old, so at least he was spared the thankless task of fund-raising to keep out the elements. It was while he was at North Holmwood that he first applied his literary talents to writing hymns.

In 1900, when he was 45, he became vicar of St. Augustin's in Bournemouth, a town of many beautiful churches. 90 years earlier it was a completely deserted stretch of coastline, and even in 1860 the population was under 2,000. But by the time Lowry arrived it had risen to about 60,000, and by the time he died in 1932 that figure had doubled.

Arthur Mee describes Bournemouth as "the sort of town that will always attract men and women with imagination and a love of romantic beauty." It certainly attracted Robert Louis Stevenson, and John Keble the hymn-writer, and the naturalist W.H. Hudson, and another hymn-writer, Canon Twells, author of "At even, ere the sun was set." All these men spent their final years at Bournemouth.

The town has six miles of bathing beaches, a million flowers, thousands of fragrant pines and lovely surroundings in all directions, making it a veritable garden city by the sea. After his early years in Doncaster, Somerset Lowry must have thought he had arrived in heaven – with all due respects to Doncaster, which has much to commend it, but not a million flowers!

Ten years before Lowry's arrival, the great statesman W.E. Gladstone made his last communion in another Bournemouth church, St. Peter's, while staying in the town for his health. He was clearly near his end, and word got out that he wanted to die at Hawarden, his home.

When he reached the station he found a large crowd assembled, and as he walked with brave steps along the platform, someone called out, "God bless you, sir!" He turned to face the crowd, took off his hat, and in a firm, deep voice replied, "God bless you all, and this place, and the land we love."

As vicar of St. Augustin's Lowry is likely to have found in his congregation many interesting people, and a large proportion of them retired folk. He continued with his hymn-writing and wrote two for use in times of war, "Behold, Lord, how the nations rage" for the Russian and Japanese conflict of 1904, and "Lord, while afar our brothers fight" written at Holmwood during the Boer War.

He also wrote a hymn for Queen Victoria's annual memorial service for Prince Albert, and "We meet as we have never met before" which was specifically for a child's funeral at Holmwood. His prose works included two highly respected publications, 'Lessons from the Passion' and 'The Work of the Holy Spirit'.

"A Man there lived in Galilee" was written probably when Lowry was at St. Augustin's, Bournemouth, and came to public attention when it was included by 'Hymns Ancient and Modern' in their 1969 supplement, '100 Hymns for Today'. The three verses depict the life of Jesus in Galilee, his death and our salvation at Calvary and his continuing reign in glory. It thus traces a basic Christian theology in simple terms that can be immediately understood by Christians of all ages and persuasions.

The first verse goes:

> "A Man there lived in Galilee
> Unlike all men before,
> For he alone from first to last
> Our flesh unsullied wore;
> A perfect life of perfect deeds
> Once to the world was shown,
> That all mankind might mark his steps
> And in them plant their own."

The tune used for this hymn is a Tyrolean melody. It is a jaunty tune with a firm rhythm which is heartily invigorating to sing. This cheerful, happy tune suggests joy in the salvation of our sins and the knowledge of Our Lord's continuing care for us from the heavenly kingdom.

The balmy climate of Bournemouth clearly suited Somerset Lowry, as it has so many folk who have retired there. He lived to be 77 and died in 1932.

WILLIAM HENRY DRAPER
"All creatures of our God and King"

William Henry Draper was a scholar and Church of England clergyman of the High Church tradition, who combined his ministry in busy parishes in the Midlands and north of England with his passion for writing hymns. He wrote over 60 in all, including some first rate translations from the Latin and Greek.

The most famous is "All creatures of our God and King," written when he was rector of Adel, near Leeds, for a Whitsunday festival for children, held in Leeds early in the 20th century. It is an exultant hymn of praise, a free translation of the 'Canticle of the Creatures', written by St. Francis of Assisi. The first four verses were probably written by the saint after a period of 40 days and 40 nights, communing very close to nature in his ramshackle hut at San Damiano.

He had renounced all his earthly riches and was living in utter poverty, with birds hopping in and out, rats scuttling about in the shadows during the hours of darkness and rain soaking his blanket. In this basic habitation he was able to witness the beauty of God's creation.

Apart from the creatures, St. Francis made mention of the burning sun, the silver moon, the rushing wind and the clouds that sail in heaven. He did not forget the lights of the evening, the flowing water and the fire "so masterful and bright." Finally he came to the flowers and fruits, that gave him such delight in his vigil of solitude.

It needed a poet and a scholar of unusual sensitivity to translate this Latin poem into an equally joyous English hymn, and William Draper was that man. He must have had Psalm 148 very much in mind when he embarked upon his translation in his study at Adel. The psalm begins:

"O praise the Lord of heaven: praise him in the height.
Praise him, all ye angels of his: praise him all his host.
Praise him, sun and moon: praise him, all ye stars and light."

The rousing tune that so fittingly captures the joyous nature of this hymn of praise is surely one that the gentle St. Francis would have sung in his hut with the sheer exuberance of being alive, had it not been written some 400 years after his death. It is 'Laast Uns Erfreuen' which first appeared in Cologne in 1623. The 'English Hymnal' first introduced it to Britain, early in the 20th century.

William Draper was born at Kenilworth in 1855, in the shadow of the old castle that dominates the town. Perhaps it is not surprising that he spent much of his life studying old manuscripts and officiating in old churches, for a sense of history must have pervaded his home. He was the son of Henry and Lucy Mary Draper.

William received his classical education at Keble College, Oxford, where he graduated BA with honours. He had no doubts about what he wanted to do with his life, and at the age of 24 he was ordained. In 1880 he embarked on his first curacy, at St. Mary's Church, Shrewsbury.

He was a keen supporter of the Oxford Movement, which would have pleased the founder of his college. The Movement was a High Church resurgence, aiming to abolish much of the indifference and laxity that had crept into the Church of England, and to re-establish the traditional liturgy of the ancient church. St. Mary's, Shrewsbury, had a High Church tradition.

The church is mentioned in the Domesday Book, and indeed has examples of every style of English architecture from the 12th to 17th centuries. It contains some exquisite stained glass, some originally from the Abbey of Treves and more from the Abbey of Herckenrode, in Belgium. In 1894 the summit of the 200 foot spire came crashing down in a storm on to the roof of the nave, which it destroyed. Fortunately for the young curate, he had left a few years previously.

From St. Mary's, Draper moved eastwards across the country to take up his appointment as vicar of Alfreton. It is an attractive town in the flatter, eastern part of Derbyshire, close to what was once the mining district. But Shrewsbury did not forget him, and when the incumbency at the Abbey Church fell vacant, William Draper was invited to take the post.

This he did, for the Abbey Church is also the parish church of Holy Cross, and is rich in the atmosphere of ancient prayer. It was once the nave of the Abbey of St. Peter and St. Paul, founded by Roger Montgomery in 1083. At the east end of the church are some massive Norman pillars.

In 1899, when he was still only 44, Draper moved once more, to become rector of Adel, near Leeds. Perhaps he was caught up in the social and economic changes of the times, and considered Shrewsbury to be too comfortable a berth as heavy industry dominated so many people's lives further north and east.

Leeds for centuries had been dominated by the Nonconformist Churches, but a remarkable ministry by Dr. Hook earlier in the 19th century had completely transformed it into a stronghold of the Church of England. Cosmo Gordon Lang, the future Archbishop of Canterbury, went to the Parish Church there as a curate just a few years before Draper arrived at Adel. Lang reckoned his time at Leeds, working in the appalling slums, was the happiest in his life.

Draper never considered his hymns and sacred verse of much consequence, and never collected them into a single volume. They appeared in such publications as 'The Guardian' and 'Church Monthly', from where they were picked up by various editors of hymnals. Several of his hymns were included in the 'Council Schools Hymn Book', and another two in 'Hymns in Times of War'.

He wrote a national hymn for the coronation of Edward VII, and another for a choral festival in Gloucester Cathedral. As his reputation as a hymn-writer grew, his work was picked up by the editor of 'Hymns Ancient and Modern'.

ADEL CHURCH in 1908, when William Henry Draper was its rector.

"Lord, through this Holy Week of our salvation" was written for 'Hymns for Holy Week', and other work followed for the 'Victoria Book of Hymns'.

But his masterpiece is undoubtedly "All creatures of our God and King," that inspired translation of a saint's work, who witnessed the full glory of nature from his hut in Italy. St. Francis and William Draper would have found a lot in common, not least a deep love of beauty.

Draper became very fond of the little village of Adel, and especially of its Norman church, which he lovingly restored at a cost of £1,332. In fact he wrote a weighty volume on it, which contains the following description of the old building:

"The outside of the building, excepting the porch and the corbels, has but little form or comeliness, no great length or height, no rugged tower or sky-pointing spire, no traceried windows, or anything which from a distance can charm the eye; but the moment one steps inside the door and turns towards the east, the impression of the whole comes with an arresting power, like that of some grave and uncommon face, showing the handwriting of heaven. You are aware that you see the whole of the church at once, that there will be no aisles to explore, no transepts to wander into, no recesses to penetrate; and yet the sense which this imparts is not that of littleness so much as solemnity, not that of restriction but of completeness: it is known to you immediately as a House of God, where questions of size are nothing and the suggestion of the Presence is everything."

DOROTHY FRANCES GURNEY
"O perfect love, all human love transcending"

Dorothy Gurney was born at Finsbury Circus in London in 1858. Her father, the Rev'd. Frederick Blomfield, was rector of St. Andrew's Undershaft, in the City of London, and her grandfather had been a former Bishop of London. Dorothy had three younger sisters – Katherine, Isabella and Daisy – and a younger brother, Frederick.

As a girl Dorothy was rather retiring, not the kind of child who would enjoy the attentions of her father's Sunday morning congregation telling her how she had grown, or commenting on how pretty her frock was. She longed for the seclusion of the rectory garden, where she could plant her seeds and watch them germinate, or feel at home with the changing seasons of nature.

She started writing verse when still a young girl, and clearly won for herself a reputation among family and friends for the quality of her poetry. One of her poems that later on was acclaimed far and wide is 'God's Garden', with the intriguing first verse:

> "The Lord God planted a garden
> In the first white days of the world,
> And he set there an angel warden
> In a garden of white enfurled."

In due course all three of Dorothy's younger sisters married and moved away, leaving Dorothy still at home with her parents. She seemed destined to have the task of looking after them as they slipped into old age, living out a life of devout spinsterhood. But when she was 39 her life took an unexpected turn.

She fell in love with Gerald Gurney, the eldest son of the vicar of Hambledon, near Henley- on- Thames. The vicar was the Rev'd. Archer Thompson Gurney, a prolific hymn-writer in his own right. Gerald was four years younger than Dorothy, but he had enjoyed a far less secluded existence than she had before they met.

When he came down from Oxford Gerald became an actor, a profession that was not deemed respectable in Victorian times and was particularly unsuitable for the son of a respected clergyman. His parents at the Oxfordshire vicarage, hoping that their oldest son would follow in the ecclesiastical tradition, must have been perturbed. But their worries were assuaged shortly before he met Dorothy, for he had a change of heart and became ordained.

Dorothy and Gerald were duly married, and Gerald started his own ministry in the Church of England which was to last for 22 years. But as time went on, both became quietly disillusioned with the secular side of the Established Church, and like the adherents to the Oxford Movement half a century before, yearned after the more strictly spiritual teaching of the Roman Catholic Church at that time. Both were received into the Church of Rome in 1919, which necessitated Gerald giving up his living.

This was a big decision for them, as they knew it would disappoint and even shock many of their friends and family. But Dorothy was held in such high regard by her true friends because she had a great fount of sympathy for her fellow humans. She was a repository for other people's troubles, and friends both rich and poor brought to her their cares and concerns. They knew that they would receive from her a sympathetic hearing. She also had a quiet, infectious sense of humour, so many who came to her with long faces went away smiling.

Dorothy Gurney's only known hymn is the still very popular wedding hymn, "O perfect love, all human love transcending." She wrote it at Brathay, just south of Ambleside in the Lake District, in 1883 when she was 25. Her younger sister Katherine was about to marry the son of a local land-owner, and the wedding was fast approaching.

One Sunday evening in mid-winter the family had gathered together to sing hymns round the harmonium, and Katherine was particularly concerned with finding suitable hymns for her wedding. Her favourite tune was J.B. Dykes's rendering for "O strength and stay," a fine hymn from the 4th century by St. Ambrose, which had recently been translated into English by John Ellerton.

Not surprisingly, however, she found the words unsuitable for a wedding. One line reads, "The brightness of a holy death-bed blending," which was not the image Katherine wanted to contemplate on her wedding day.

So in some frustration she turned to Dorothy and said, "What's the use of having a sister who's a poet if she can't write me a hymn for my wedding?" Dorothy took the rebuke seriously, although it was no doubt delivered in jest. She picked up her notebook and pencil and left the room. Not long later she reappeared with her new hymn, written specially for Katherine and Hugh, her future husband, which starts:

> "O perfect love, all human thought transcending,
> Lowly we kneel in prayer before thy throne."

It was duly sung at Brathay Church to the tune of John Bacchus Dykes, precentor of Durham Cathedral. The hymn became immensely popular when 'Hymns Ancient and Modern' published it in their supplement six years after the wedding. It received a further boost when Princess Louise, Queen Victoria's grand-daughter, chose it for her wedding. It was then published and sung on countless occasions, and each time its author should have received a royalty. In actual fact she never received a penny, for she never claimed the copyright protection.

Most hymnals today set it to the tune 'Sandringham' by Sir Joseph Barnby, a Yorkshireman who was principal of the Guildhall School of Music. An alternative preferred by 'The English Hymnal' and 'Songs of Praise' is 'Welwyn', by A. Scott-Gatty.

As a girl spending regular family holidays at Ambleside, Dorothy is quite likely to have come across Harriet Martineau, who moved to the town in 1844. She was a prolific writer, and organised to no small extent the affairs of the little Westmorland town.

Harriet read 'Paradise Lost' when she was seven, and came to know it almost by heart. As a girl she was very religious in a strictly practical manner, but changed her beliefs later. As Norman Nicholson memorably described her, "She looked on God, from childhood, as a schoolmaster giving instruction and correcting homework, and later, when she believed that she had learnt the rules, she was quite ready to manage her curriculum without Him!"

Miss Martineau built for herself The Knoll, just out of town on the road to Grasmere, where she dug a pit in the garden close to the Methodist Chapel for her daily bath, taken when the neighbours were still fast asleep. She also started a dairy herd, in the safe hands of her own dairyman who came with her from her native Norfolk.

Harriet considered it her duty to attend to the education of Ambleside. The village children were instructed on various topics and used her garden as a playground. The working population was treated to a series of lectures on English history, America, the Crimean War and sanitation. When she moved on to the dangers of alcohol, her diagrams of the decay of the lining of the stomach were so lurid that one local fellow, notorious for his fondness of the bottle, hurried outside to be sick.

Many famous literary names came to visit her at The Knoll, none more regularly than her neighbour William Wordsworth, who planted a tree in her garden. Others included George Eliot, Emerson, Elizabeth Gaskell, Catherine Winkworth, Hallam, Sydney Smith, Carlyle and Henry Hart Milman, the Dean of St. Paul's. Another who thoroughly enjoyed her stay in the spare room was Charlotte Bronte, who came shortly after the tragic deaths of her sisters Emily and Ann and her brother Branwell.

Dorothy would have been sixteen when Harriet Martineau died in 1874, and already writing verse. She may well have walked over to The Knoll and bellowed into the enormous ear-trumpet, for Harriet was almost totally deaf. It would have been very unlike Harriet to overlook a literary talent blossoming on her own doorstep.

Those carefree holidays in the Lake District would have become a dim memory to Dorothy as she progressed towards old age amidst the London city streets. She and Gerald were a devoted couple to the last. She died at Kensington in 1932 aged 74, and Gerald lived on in London for a further ten years.

GEORGE BENNARD
"On a hill far away stood an old rugged cross"

George Bennard has acquired a place in the history of hymnology through having written both words and music of one of the great classics of revivalist mission meetings. This is the immortal hymn 'The Old Rugged Cross'.

He was born in Youngstown, between Pittsburg and Cleveland in Ohio, where his father was a coalminer. During George's childhood the family moved first to Albia and then to Lucas, both in Iowa, following the trail of where mining work was available. Times were tough and life was hard, so when his father died although George was only fifteen, he had to support his mother and sisters as best he could.

Amidst the smoke and grime of the industrial towns, the mission meetings were the one gleam of light for the impressionable teenager. He longed to become an evangelist himself, and at Lucas he joined the Salvation Army. Publicly acknowledging Christ as his Saviour, he spent all his spare time at their gatherings. He married a girl who was as ardent in her faith as he was, and both worked for the Salvation Army in Illinois.

As a young man he was ordained into the Methodist Episcopal Church, and was active at revivalist meetings in Michigan and New York State. It was for these missions that he started writing and composing his hymns and music. He wrote over 300 in his lifetime, and one of them achieved an enduring reputation throughout the world..

He wrote 'The Old Rugged Cross' in 1913 when he was in a mental state of some anguish, possibly after having to endure an unpleasant experience at one of his meetings. All evangelists have to cope with these from time to time. Even the great John Wesley was quite badly injured on one visit to Bolton, when he was punched in the face and pelted with stones.

George Bennard was contemplating St. Paul's remark about entering into the fellowship of Christ's suffering, and his thoughts kept recurring to the cross. He realised that this was the focal point of all Christianity, and he determined to write a hymn with the cross as its theme.

At the time he was staying at the house of Prof. Delos Fall in Albion, Michigan. The professor rented out rooms, and Bennard was staying in one of them for the duration of his mission. He sat down and wrote the melody first, which came to him almost at once. But the words would not form themselves in his mind. He kept looking at his pad, but all he had written was "I'll cherish the old rugged cross." For weeks he tried to find inspiration, but it would not come.

He had this picture in his mind of the cross as a hulk of rough, splintery wood, stained with blood and ugly to behold. The gilted, beautifully crafted crosses that adorned churches he considered to be totally false images.

Then one day he came in from his day's work, took up his pad and pencil again and the words flowed. He told a friend later, "I sat down and immediately was able to rewrite the stanzas of the song without so much as one word failing to fall into place. I called in my wife, took out my guitar, and sang the completed song to her. She was thrilled!"

Bennard first introduced his new hymn to a revivalist gathering at Pokagon, Michigan, where it was received with gleeful acclaim. Not long afterwards it was sung by a huge congregation at the Chicago Evangelistic Institute. This launched it to the American public, and very soon it was in the top ten of favourite hymns. It remained there for most of the 20th century, often reaching the number one spot.

An incredible 20 million copies were sold in its first 30 years. It was whistled and hummed and sung by all sections of society, in every continent.

The hymn has probably had more religious appeal than all the sermons delivered during his lifetime.

Had he wished it, George Bennard could have amassed an enormous fortune from this one hymn. In fact, he sold the copyright for a mere $500 to the Rodeheaver Company of Winona Lake, Indiana. At least he did better than Julia Ward Howe, who received just four dollars for all rights to her masterpiece, "Mine eyes have seen the glory of the coming of the Lord."
In those days, the success of a song or hymn was determined by the number of copies it sold, and the popularity of 'The Old Rugged Cross' was phenomenal. It was as popular as any piece of contemporary secular music and the name of George Bennard was known by almost every American Christian. As for the author, he continued with his gospel missions until half way through the 20th century, by which time he was an octogenarian.

He wrote a vast number of other songs and hymns and composed the music to go with them, including "Speak, my Lord" and "Tell me his name again." Several were popular, but none achieved anything like the acclaim of his masterpiece. Bennard operated a music company and tract society in downtown Albion for many years, a town to the west of Detroit. Even when the house where he wrote 'The Old Rugged Cross' was demolished, the song was commemorated by a series of telephone poles erected as rugged crosses.

George Bennard was often invited to appear as a celebrity at revivalist gatherings, but the chairmen of these meetings were sometimes lax in their homework. As the years rolled on he used to joke that he had been introduced, on various occasions, as the author of 'The Old Grey Mare', 'The Old Oaken Bucket', and even 'Rock of Ages', whose actual author, Augustus Toplady, died in 1778. On one occasion he was even presented to the congregation as George Bennard Shaw!

He spent his retirement years a short distance from Reed City, Michigan, where he died in 1958, aged 85. A large cross still stands on the spot, erected by the local chamber of commerce. It bears the inscription: "The Old Rugged Cross – home of George Bennard, composer of this beloved hymn." No doubt to this day many a traveller will sing the famous refrain as he or she motors past:

"So I'll cherish the old rugged cross,
Till my trophies at last I lay down;
I will cling to the old rugged cross
And exchange it some day for a crown."

The life of George Bennard is commemorated at a museum in Reed City, The Old Rugged Cross Historical Museum. He was buried at Inglewood Park Cemetery at Inglewood in California.

JAN STRUTHER
"When a knight won his spurs in the stories of old"

As a young boy growing up in England in the 1940s, I always hoped that we would sing this hymn at Sunday school. The romantic picture of a mounted knight, armed with lance and shield, galloping about the countryside in the service of God and valour was immensely appealing. It was an age when we still had well-thumbed volumes of 'The Knights of King Arthur' on our bedroom bookshelves, along with the latest football and cricket annuals.

"When a knight won his spurs" is an example of what Percy Dearmer thought Jan Struther, its author, did so well. There is no real religious theology in the hymn, yet it commands the Christian virtues of gentleness, bravery, faith and truth. It stands for all that is right, yet one does not need to be a Christian to affirm its sentiments.

Percy Dearmer, featured in Volume 2 of this series, was so impressed by the sensitivity of Jan Struther's verse that he asked her to contribute some hymns to the 1925 edition of 'Songs of Praise', which he was editing. He was also the chief editor of 'The English Hymnal', published in 1906. Dearmer knew that Jan Struther was not a Christian, but he was producing a hymnal that was less conventional than most. He rightly assessed that her poetry would appeal to people who were not overtly religious, but nevertheless treasured ethics and sentiments that were spiritual in tone.

F.R. Barry, Dearmer's next-door neighbour in London, wrote about 'Songs of Praise': "Its aim was to offer the congregations – who took their theology mainly from the hymns – a virile, outward-looking presentation of the Christian faith for the new age, freed from some of the weak, mawkish sentiments which had crept into the 19th century hymn-books." A free-thinker who refused to be bound by conventions, such as Jan Struther, was just the kind of author he cherished.

"When a knight won his spurs" still appears in 'Enlarged Songs of Praise' and 'Hymns Old and New'. The tune to which it is invariably sung is a traditional English melody called 'Stowey', arranged and harmonised by Ralph Vaughan Williams. It complements the poem perfectly, with a whimsical nostalgia for the chargers of old, and a sad acceptance that romanticism is over – "The knights are no more and the dragons are dead."

Jan Struther was born in London in 1901. Her maiden name was Anstruther, from which she derived her pen-name of Jan Struther. Her actual name was Mrs Joyce Placzek, but when she decided to make writing her career she chose a pseudonym that was rather easier to recall. She wrote a good deal of challenging poetry, full of controversial ideas and images, and this appeared in periodicals on both sides of the Atlantic.

She also wrote a novel, 'Mrs Miniver', which was converted into a most successful film in 1939. It captured the public mood for escapism in the early months of the war, when the question on everybody's lips was "Have you seen 'Mrs Miniver' yet?"

Jan emigrated to America where her first marriage proved to be something of a disaster. But later in her life she fell in love again, and left her roots to pursue her new-found happiness. At length she was married for the second time, but sadly the couple were not destined to enjoy each other's company for very long. Jan died at the age of 52 in 1951.

Another of Jan Struther's contributions to 'Songs of Praise' was "Lord of all hopefulness, Lord of all joy." She wrote it at the request of Percy Dearmer to go with the tune 'Slane', the Irish melody that is normally associated with "Be thou my vision." Cyril Taylor, one time precentor at Bristol Cathedral and chaplain to the Royal School of Church Music, thought that 'Slane' should be reserved solely for "Be thou my vision," so he set about composing an alternative tune. This he appropriately called 'Miniver'.

Jan Struther is probably the only hymn-writer in this series of books who would not have accepted the Creed. But in her love of humanity and appreciation of beauty there was plenty of spirituality in her soul.

FRED PRATT GREEN
"For the fruits of his creation"

One of the best known names in modern hymnology is that of Fred Pratt Green, the Methodist minister who wrote over 300 hymns in the second half of the 20th century. 40 or so years ago there was a movement to create new hymns, sometimes in modern verse format, as an alternative to the more traditional hymns that were to be found in mid-20th century hymnals. Fred Pratt Green was one of the leaders of this movement, and his hymns have certainly retained their popularity.

The theology and ideas in his hymns are always expressed in a clear, stark, easily understood manner, and are challenging because they are relevant to contemporary affairs. Frequent themes are justice, sharing our resources and our responsibility to those less fortunate than ourselves. If he were alive today he would be writing about global warming, poverty in Africa and a fair trade policy. His hymns are full of basic common sense, which indeed sums up his own personality.

Fred was born in 1903 at the east Liverpool district of Roby. The family moved across the Mersey to Wallasey and then to the Manchester area. It was there, at Didsbury College, that he received most of his education. When he was 25 he was ordained into the Methodist ministry, and for the next 42 years he was a dedicated minister in various parts of the country. It is not Methodist policy to keep their ministers in the same place for very long.

Fred Pratt Green retired in 1969 when he was 66, and instead of acting as a minister he became a prolific hymn-writer. Throughout his ministry he had written plays and poems, some of which he used in services or social events connected with his churches. Now he followed in the steps of that other great Methodist hymnologist, Charles Wesley, who during his life wrote 6,500 hymns.

The 'United Methodist Hymnal' contains fifteen of Fred Green's hymns, and two more translations. They are also really popular in North America, where the editors of English-speaking hymnals have taken a great liking to his work.

One of the more traditional and most popular of his hymns is "For the fruits of his creation," first published in the 'Methodist Recorder' in 1970. It starts as a simple hymn of thanksgiving for the harvest:

> "For the ploughing, sowing, reaping,
>   Silent growth while we are sleeping."

It goes on to acknowledge the just reward of labour, and to remind us of our duty to care for those who cannot rely on a regular harvest because of droughts and other extremes of nature. It suggests by implication how important it is to adopt a fair trade policy for the developing world, and then finally it refers to the "harvests of the Spirit," the intangible harvest that produces abundant love.

The words were written for the tune 'East Acklam', composed in 1957 by Francis Jackson. The traditional Welsh melody 'Ar Hyd y Nos' is also sometimes used, although this tune is normally associated with Reginald Heber's hymn, "God that madest earth and heaven."

As one would expect from a 20th century north countryman, there is nothing sentimental about either Fred or his hymns. He once remarked about hymn-singing: "It's such a dangerous activity... You get this glow which you can mistake for religious experience." He was a pragmatist with a warm heart and a caring spirit, whom people warmed to immediately.

He finally settled in Norwich, where he died in 2000 at the grand old age of 97.

FRED KAAN
"For the healing of the nations"

When Fred Kaan was a young Congregational minister working in Plymouth in the early 1960s, he could not find hymns that were relevant to the problems and issues of the day. 'The Congregational Hymnary' of that time was an excellent hymnal with well over 700 hymns in it, but a lot of them were from the previous century or before.

His hymn "Sing we of the modern city" was written in a fit of frustration after reading the hymn "Sing we of the golden city pictured in the legends old; everlasting light shines o'er it, wondrous tales of it are told," by the late Victorian writer, Felix Adler. "What on earth," he mused, "does this mean to a single teenage mum with a baby in a push-chair, living on the fourteenth floor of an apartment block where the lift isn't working?"

Kaan therefore decided he would have to write his own hymns, about the issues he and his congregation had to face every day of their working lives. The result was his own production of a supplement called 'Pilgrim Praise'. Since that time Fred Kaan has continued with his hymn-writing, and today all the well known modern hymnals will contain a number of popular hymns by him. They are full of contemporary recurrent themes, such as sharing our resources, caring for our planet, putting an end to exploitation, condemning hunger and poverty to history and abolishing dominance through power and might.

These are all issues that Fred Kaan feels strongly about, and as in his work he has visited over 80 countries, his experience of man's inhumanity to man (and women) is unique. All his hymns have a powerful message, and some of his lines and phrases stay in the memory long after the service is over, because they are so potent. "Changing tears to laughter" is one, and "We cry for the plight of the hungry" is another. A gardening metaphor that sadly never seems to lose its relevance is "Teach us to coax the plant of peace to flower."

"For the healing of the nations" was written in the 1960s when Kaan was working in Plymouth, and the chill and fear of the cold war comes across in its verses. Despair, fear, war and hatred all occur in verse two, for the threat of the nuclear bomb was real enough. This is one of the hymns in which Kaan pleads for fair sharing of the earth's good things. Exploitation of the poor nations by the rich ones as well as corporate and private greed were in vogue then as much as they are today.

Fred Kaan was born in a terraced house in Haarlem, Holland, in 1929. It is hardly surprising that he has been a passionate pacifist all his life, for he was a schoolboy when the Germans invaded his country and few people in England today will have seen at such close quarters the atrocities of life under a Nazi regime. The Kaan family had moved to Zeist, a small town near Utrecht, at the time of the invasion when Fred was aged eleven.

His father Hermanus and mother Brandina were both staunch socialists and very much involved in the Dutch Resistance movement. In two years during the occupation 107,000 Dutch Jews were exterminated by the Nazis. The full horror of the situation was brought home to young Fred when close friends of his who lived just down the street were taken away in the middle of the night.

Hermanus and Brandina sat down with Fred and his brother Herman to explain to them that they had decided to offer a hideaway in their house to a Jewish lawyer, called Philine Polak. This was an incredibly courageous decision, for they would be sent to a labour camp if they were found out. One unguarded remark at school or in the shops could have broken up the family circle for ever.

There was a vacant space in their new house underneath the stairs leading from the first to the second floors and concealed between two wardrobes. They constructed a door that could only be opened from the inside, and cushioned the floor with mattresses. Hermanus then went to see his Dutch Resistance leader and friend Hannie Schaft, to report that they were ready to receive a Jew. Hannie decided that Philine, a young university friend of hers, should take refuge there.

She lived with the Kaans for two-and-a-half years, joining them for meals and helping the boys with their homework. Fred and his brother Herman listened in awe as she and her father earnestly discussed a range of humanitarian and Resistance issues, and they became close friends. Sometimes in the dead of night Hermanus would take Philine to the copse over the road for a walk, their way lit up by the bombing raids that were never far away. Several times their house was raided by the Gestapo, but they never discovered the secret hiding-place.

Poor Philine became more and more frustrated, cooped up in her claustrophobic sanctuary, as the months slipped past. Finally she could stand it no longer. Clad in her overcoat, the collar turned up to conceal as much as she could of her unmistakably Jewish profile, she slipped out into the night and made for Amsterdam. There she planned to meet up again with Hannie Schaft, the Resistance leader who was her close friend. And for 60 years that was the last Fred heard of her.

The Kaan family knew that Hannie was captured by the Nazis in 1944 and shot. They assumed that the same fate had overtaken Philine. But in 2004 Dr. Gillian Warson started work on a biography of Fred, and was intrigued by the story of Philine. Painstakingly she pursued a detective trail using the internet, and finally after many setbacks she obtained the address of a Philine Polak-Lachman from a web site about the life of Hannie Schaft. Philine was living in Maine, USA, and was due to attend a commemoration event in Haarlem late in 2005, in memory of Hannie.

Fred and Dr. Warson attended the commemoration and so he was able once again to meet up with his childhood house-guest from war-time Holland. Philine is grey-haired and very slight now, but the great joy and exhilaration at seeing each other again after 60 years can, perhaps, only be fully appreciated by those few who have been through such a unique experience together.

Fred Kaan originally intended to enter art school after his school education in Zeist, but he changed his mind after living under Nazi occupation for five years. Three of his grandparents died of starvation in the winter of misery that followed the Battle of Arnhem, and by the time the war was over he was a committed pacifist.

DR. FRED KAAN

He became interested in religion, and mainly as a result of corresponding with a young Congregational pen-friend in Essex, he applied to enter a Congregationalist theological college in Bristol. He was accepted, and in 1952 at the age of 23 he started his theological studies there.

Dr. Kaan was ordained in 1955 and was inducted to his first pastorate at Windsor Road Congregational Church in Barry, South Wales, among the coalminers and steel workers. After eight invigorating years there he moved on to a pastorate at the Pilgrim Congregational Church in Plymouth, which he describes as providing the most exciting experiences of his entire ministry. The Plymouth folk were the most imaginative, warm and original people he ever worked with, and together they explored the writing of new and original hymns. They were wholly committed to serving the world both locally and internationally, a true Church Universal. Whilst there he produced his first collection of hymns, 'Pilgrim Praise'.

His next move, in 1968, was to Geneva, where he was appointed minister-secretary at the International Congregational Council, which merged with the World Alliance of Reformed Churches two years later. He did much valuable work on their international hymnal, 'Cantate Domino', and his linguistic ability was put to good use. Dr. Kaan's liberal, forward-looking ideas and zealous, crusading principles made him a valuable ambassador for the Alliance, and he visited more than 80 countries in his ten years there. His love of people made him a most popular guest wherever he went.

In 1978 Fred Kaan returned to England as Moderator of the West Midlands Province of the United Reformed Church, and seven years later he moved on to a United Reformed church in Swindon. As the years moved on, he found himself spending more and more of his time in public speaking. In retirement he became secretary of the Churches' Human Rights forum in 1993, the year that also sadly saw the death of his first wife, Elly Steller.

Dr. Kaan and his second wife, Anthea Cooke, now live in the Lake District, where Anthea acted as the local GP until she retired. She started her medical career at a hospital in Madras before spending most of her working life in Birmingham, latterly as senior partner at an inner city medical centre with 7,000 multi-racial patients.

Daughters-in-law come from Sweden and Hungary, and relatives from the first marriage live in Germany and Holland, so the international flavour of Fred's life continues to engulf him. In fact, he and his wife can converse in nine languages between them, plus the classical tongues of Latin, Greek and Hebrew.

Both of them spend their retirement in taking every available action to bring about peace in every corner of the earth. They march, write letters of protest and will continue to march with millions of like-minded people. Fred continues to write hymns, translate hymns, make friends, travel all over the world and lecture in every continent. At the age of 76 he acts like a 30 year old.

He has written over 200 hymns since starting in his Plymouth days, some of which have been translated into over fifteen languages. The most recent collection of them is 'The Only Earth We Know', published in 1999. Probably the best known of his hymns is "For the healing of the nations," written to celebrate Human Rights Day in 1965 at the Pilgrim Church in Plymouth. It has been chosen for many international and state occasions both at home and abroad, including the 25th anniversary of the United Nations.

It is a very powerful hymn, full of the need to love and share, and pleading for an end to war and fear. The tune most often used for it is 'Grafton', a traditional French melody. Fred Kaan's hymns are not only the very best crafted examples of modern hymnody but also valuable insights into the social problems of the human race in the 20th and 21st centuries.

So Fred Kaan and his wife Dr. Anthea take their places alongside eminent figures who have found their ultimate home amidst the hills and dales of the Lake District. The list is a long one. William Wordsworth, Samuel Coleridge, Robert Southey, Matthew Arnold, Harriet Martineau, Beatrix Potter and Norman Nicholson represent the writers and poets. Then there were George Romney the artist and George Fox, the founder of the Quakers. All would have exulted in the peace and grandeur of this most beautiful part of England, and they would have shared with Fred Kaan and Anthea an abhorrence of man's inhumanity to man.

GRAHAM A. KENDRICK
"Beauty for brokenness"

No less than 37 hymns in 'Complete Anglican Hymns Old and New' are by Graham Kendrick, more than by any other hymn-writer apart from Michael Forster. He is one of the new era of hymn-writers that emerged in the 1970s when congregations were restless for more contemporary words and music than that provided by the traditional church hymnals.

The Beatles were all the rage, every teenager had a guitar on the bedroom wall and young churchgoers needed something more meaningful to their lives than "Rock of ages, cleft for me" which was top of their grandmothers' list of favourites. It was a respectful revolution, in line with peace marches, human rights demonstrations and the widening domains of an exciting new world.

Graham Kendrick was born in 1950 at Blisworth, near Northampton, where his father was pastor of the Baptist Church. The stories read to him by his mother at an early age sowed in him a strong Christian commitment, and Sunday school at his father's church nurtured his faith. After school he entered a teacher training college, but at the end of the course it was music that he intended to pursue as his Christian ministry.

When Graham was 26 he married Jill, and their four daughters complete the family. In the same year, 1976, he became musical director of the British Youth for Christ movement, a post he held for four years. He then set up the Kendrick and Stevenson music and mime duo and later became a member for a while of the leadership team of the Ichthus Christian Fellowship. In 1987 he was co-founder of the March for Jesus young Christians movement.

He has to his name a vast output of songs and hymns as well as albums that have been produced in many languages. Some of his work is certainly in the category of Christian youth camp gatherings or worship songs, with frequent repetitions and two-way repartee between leader and congregation. It is exciting and invigorating, aimed at the spontaneous stirring of emotions. One of his hymns starts:

"Come on, let's get up and go.
Let ev'ryone know."

(Extract taken from the song 'Let's Get Up and Go' by Graham Kendrick.
Copyright © 1986 Thankyou Music*)

Another is an invocation to joy:

"The King is among us,
His spirit is here,
Let's draw near and worship
Let songs fill the air."

(Extract from the song 'The King is Coming' by Graham Kendrick.
Copyright © 1981 Thankyou Music*)

But others are far more substantial, addressing the real issues that beset our
world. A moving and very powerful hymn is his "Beauty for brokenness,"
which contains in verse 3 the following lines:

"Peace to the killing fields,
Scorched earth to green,
Christ for the bitterness
His cross for the pain."

(Graham Kendrick © 1993 Make Way Music. wwwgrahamkendrick.co.uk)

Graham Kendrick's own favourite is 'The Servant King', which has as its
first line, "From heav'n you came, helpless Babe." The chorus goes:

"This is our God, the Servant King,
He calls us now to follow him."

(Extract taken from the song 'The Servant King by Graham Kendrick.
Copyright © 1983 Thank You Music*)

Music was often to be heard in the Kendrick household, as Graham
Kendrick's father and his brothers were musical. Graham himself spent his
early years receiving piano lessons, until he claims that his teacher gave up
on him. His own children appreciate music, but do not play any instruments.

Perhaps it is not surprising that the traditional hymn-writer that Kendrick
rates most highly is Charles Wesley. The salvation of our sins through the

156

sacrifice on the cross by Our Lord is a recurrent theme in both men's hymns, although they are so different in form and technique.

Graham Kendrick has certainly contributed substantially to both branches of modern hymnody, the traditional hymn and the worship song. Ian Bradley successfully defines the difference between the two in an article written for 'The Tablet' internet pages to accompany their poll on readers' favourite hymns in 2004. He writes: "On the whole, the former is longer, cast in strophic and metrical form, often with a more objective theological perspective and generally written for accompaniment by organ or piano rather than by praise band."

There have been occasional instances of hymn-writers sitting down and writing off their lines instantaneously. Reginald Heber, for example, completed "From Greenland's icy mountains" in fifteen minutes for his step-father, the Dean of St. Asaph, who had a missionary service on the following day. Graham Kendrick admits to moments of inspiration, but adds that a lot of hard work is needed to turn it into a finished song. Sometimes inspiration comes from books or speakers, and most often these days from the Psalms.

Graham Kendrick continues to pursue his Christian ministry through that most appealing of all approaches, music. He and Jill, his wife, run their own music company, Make Way Music, based in Croydon. His hymn – or song – 'The Servant King' features in the top 20 of most contemporary lists of favourite hymns.

OTHER HYMNS BY FEATURED HYMN-WRITERS

EDMUND SPENSER — Most glorious Lord of life, that on this day

PHILIPP NICOLAI — How brightly shines the morning star!
Sleepers, wake, a voice is calling!

WILLIAM BULLOCK — We love the place, O God

ROBERT ROBINSON — Years are rolling, life is wasting
Once more with joyous greeting
Come, thou fount of every blessing
Mighty God, while angels bless thee
Beauteous scenes on earth appear
Hear, gracious God, and from thy throne
I love thy house, my Lord, my King
I've been in chase of pleasure
Now while my heart rejoices

MICHAEL BRUCE — Where high the heavenly temple stands
O happy is the man who hears

WILLIAM BLAKE — And did those feet in ancient time

THOMAS KELLY — The head that once was crowned with thorns
Grant us, Lord, thy gracious presence
Saviour, through the desert lead us
It is finished! Sinners, hear it
Jesus, the Shepherd of the sheep
Far from us be grief and sadness
Glory, glory everlasting
Happy they who trust in Jesus
Hark, the notes of angels singing
Jesus is gone up on high
Praise the Saviour, ye who know him
Gracious Lord, my heart is fixed
Lo, he comes, let all adore him
Our Father sits on yonder throne
Shepherd of the chosen number
The Lord is ris'n indeed

We sing the praise of him who died
Look, ye saints, the sight is glorious
In thy name, O Lord, assembling

HENRY KIRKE WHITE   Awake, sweet harp of Judah, wake
Christians, brethren, ere we part
Oft in danger, oft in woe
When marshalled on the mighty plain
O Lord, another day has flown
O Lord, my God, in mercy turn
The Lord our God is full of might
The Lord our God is Lord of all
Through sorrow's night and danger's path
What is this passing scene?

JOHN HAMPDEN GURNEY   Lord, as to thy dear cross we flee
Great King of nations, hear our prayer
Fair waved the golden corn
We saw thee not when thou didst come
Ye holy angels bright
Yes, God is good – in earth and sky

JOHN CHANDLER   Christ is our corner-stone
Conquering kings their titles take
On Jordan's bank the Baptist's cry
Jesus, our hope, our hearts' desire
O happy day, when first was poured
What star is this, that beams so bright
In stature grows the heavenly Child
As now the sun's declining rays
O Holy Spirit, Lord of grace

FRANCES ELIZABETH COX   Jesus lives! Thy terrors now
Who are these like stars appearing?
Sing praise to God who reigns above
O let him whose sorrow
A new and contrite heart create
Heavenward still our pathway tends
Far and near, almighty word
Come tune your heart!

159

Lo, God to heav'n ascendeth
Our blessed Saviour seven times spoke
Sleepers, wake! The watch-cry peeleth

ROBERT M. McCHEYNE   I once was a stranger to grace and to God
When this passing world is done
Beneath Moriah's rocky side
Like mist on the mountains
Ten virgins clothed in white

WILLIAM PENNEFATHER   And may I really tread
Help us, O Lord, to praise
How shall we praise thy name
Jesus, in thy blest name
Jesus, stand among us
My blessed Jesus, thou hast taught
O God of glorious majesty
O haste thy coming kingdom
O holy, holy Father
O Lord, with one accord
O Saviour, we adore thee
Once more with chastened joy
Praise God, ye seraphs bright
Thousands and thousands stand
Yon shining shore is nearer

GEORGE HUNT SMYTTAN   Forty days and forty nights
Jesu, ever present with thy Church below

WILLIAM BRIGHT   At thy feet, O Christ, we lay
And now the wants are told
And now, O Father, mindful of the love
Behold us, Lord, before thee met
How oft, O Lord, thy face hath shone
Once, only once, and once for all
We know thee, who thou art

WALTER CHALMERS SMITH Immortal, invisible, God only wise
Lord, God, Omnipotent
Our portion is not here
There is no wrath to be appeased

160

Earth was waiting, spent and restless
Faint and weary Jesus stood
If any to the feast have come
The Lord hath hid his face from us
To me to live is Christ

MARIA WILLIS   Father, hear the prayer we offer

HARRIET PARR   Hear my prayer, O Heavenly Father

ELLEN H. GATES   Come home, come home, you are weary at heart
I am now a child of God
O the clanging bells of time!
Say, is your lamp burning, my brother?
If you cannot on the ocean
I will sing you a song of that beautiful land

ELIZABETH CLEPHANE   Beneath the cross of Jesus
Dim eyes for ever closed
Who climbeth up too high
Into His summer garden
From my dwelling midst the dead
The day is drawing nearly done
Life-light waneth to an end
There were ninety and nine that safely lay

FRANCIS POTT   Angel voices ever singing
Lift up your heads, eternal gates

SAMUEL F. BENNETT   There's a land that is fairer than day

FOLLIOT S. PIERPOINT   For the beauty of the earth
O cross, O cross of shame

ARTHUR C. AINGER   God is working his purpose out
God of our fathers, unto thee
Let all our brethren join in one
Let God arise to lead forth those
Like a mighty man rejoicing in his strength
Not ours to mourn and weep
On them who here, O Lord

	Praise the Lord: today we raise
	Praise the Lord! Today we sing
WILLIAM HAY AITKEN	Bow down thine ear, in mercy harken
	O leave we all for Jesus
	Come, ye loyal hearts and true
	Father of lights, again these newborn rays
	I have sinned, thou know'st how deeply
	Let it be now, too long hast thou delayed
	Look to Jesus and be saved
	Once more, my soul
	Pitiful Saviour, mighty and tender
ROBERT BRIDGES	O sacred head, sore wounded
	All my hope on God is founded
	Thee will I love, my God and King
	Happy are they, they that love God
WILLIAM St. HILL BOURNE	Children's voices strive not vainly
	Christ, who once among us
	Enter with thanksgiving
	For the freshness of the morning
	In the name of God the Father
	The evening shadowy dimness
	The Sower went forth sowing
	Through the feeble twilight
SOMERSET C. LOWRY	A Man there lived in Galilee
	Behold, Lord, how the nations rage
	Lord, while afar our brothers fight
	O Saviour, once again the ebbing year
	O Son of God, enthroned above
	Son of God, eternal Saviour
	We meet as we have never met before
WILLIAM HENRY DRAPER	In our day of thanksgiving
	All creatures of our God and King
	Come forth, ye sick and poor
	From homes of quiet peace
	How blest the land where God is known
	How fair was the land of God's people of old

Lord, through this Holy Week of our salvation
Man shall not live by bread alone
Rejoice, ye angels in the sky
We love God's acre round the church
What can I do for England?
Ye sons of God, arise

DOROTHY F. GURNEY   O perfect love, all human thought transcending

GEORGE BENNARD   On a hill far away stood an old rugged cross
Speak, my Lord
Tell me his name again

JAN STRUTHER   Lord of all hopefulness, Lord of all joy
Round the earth a message runs
God, whose eternal mind
When a knight won his spurs in the stories of old

FRED PRATT GREEN   An upper room did our Lord prepare
Christ is the world's light, he and none other
For the fruits of his creation
Long ago, prophets knew
When, in our music

FRED KAAN   Father, who in Jesus found us
For the healing of the nations
Lord, as we rise to leave the shell of worship
Now let us from this table rise
Sing we a song of high revolt
As we break the bread
Bless, and keep us, God, in your love united
For ourselves no longer living
God! As with silent hearts we bring to mind
God! When human bonds are broken
Let us talents and tongues employ
Now join we, to praise the Creator
Out of our failure to create
Put peace into each other's hands
We turn to you, O God of ev'ry nation
We have a King who rides a donkey

GRAHAM KENDRICK   All I once held dear, built my life upon
                         At this time of giving
                         Beauty for brokenness
                         Come and see, come and see
                         Father God, we worship you
                         First light is upon our faces
                         From heav'n you came, helpless babe
                         From the sun's rising unto the sun's setting
                         Here is bread, here is wine
                         Jesus, stand among us
                         Led like a lamb to the slaughter
                         Lord, the light of your love is shining
                         Make way, make way, for Christ the King
                         May the fragrance of Jesus fill this place
                         Meekness and majesty
                         My Lord, what love is this
                         O give thanks to the Lord
                         O, heaven is in my heart
                         One shall tell another
                         Restore, O Lord
                         Such love, pure as the whitest snow
                         The King is among us
                         This is the year when hearts go free
                         We are his children, the fruit of his suff'ring
                         We believe in God the Father
                         We'll walk the land with hearts on fire
                         Who can sound the depths of sorrow
                         Who sees it all, before whose gaze
                         Can you see what we have made
                         O come and join the dance

(This list is not comprehensive in the case of every hymn-writer)

The author acknowledges as valuable source works 'A Dictionary of Hymnology' edited by Dr. John Julian, and 'The Penguin Book of Hymns' edited by Ian Bradley.